FROM THE EDITORS OF

ESSENCE

The
OBAMAS
Portrait of America's New First Family

SPECIAL INAUGURATION EDITION

Barack Obama is sworn in by Chief Justice John Roberts as the forty-fourth president of the United States before a massive crowd on the National Mall, January 20, 2009.

ESSENCE

Editor-in-Chief: Angela Burt-Murray
Executive Editor: Dawn M. Baskerville
Creative Director: Lisa Hunt
Research Chief: Christine Gordon
Design Production Manager: LaToya N. Valmont
Photo Editor: Deborah Boardley
Associate Photo Editor: Tracey Woods

THE OBAMAS: PORTRAIT OF AMERICA'S NEW FIRST FAMILY
Special Inauguration Edition

Editor: Patrik Henry Bass
Design: Alisha Neumaier
Production Manager: Carina A. Rosario
Photo Editors: Helena Ashton, Erika Yeomans
Research: Annette Rusin
Copy Editor: Hope Wright
Contributing Photographer: Scout Tufankjian

Content Credits
ESSENCE acknowledges all the writers
who contributed to this book:
Marian Wright Edelman
Charlayne Hunter-Gault
Gwen Ifill
Claire McIntosh
Isabel Wilkerson
Wendy L. Wilson

Publisher: Richard Fraiman
General Manager: Steven Sandonato
Executive Director, Marketing Services: Carol Pittard
Director, Retail & Special Sales: Tom Mifsud
Director, New Product Development: Peter Harper
Assistant Director, Newsstand Marketing: Laura Adam
Assistant Director, Brand Marketing: Joy Butts
Associate Counsel: Helen Wan
Senior Brand Manager, TWRS/M: Holly Oakes
Brand & Licensing Manager: Alexandra Bliss
Design & Prepress Manager: Anne-Michelle Gallero
Book Production Manager: Susan Chodakiewicz

Special Thanks:
Glenn Buonocore
Margaret Hess
Jennifer Jacobs
Suzanne Janso
Brynn Joyce
Robert Marasco
Brooke Reger
Mary Sarro-Waite
Ilene Schreider
Adriana Tierno
Alex Voznesenskiy

Copyright 2009
Essence Communications, Inc.
Published by Time Inc. Home
Entertainment

Time Inc.
1271 Avenue of the Americas
New York NY 10020

ISBN 13: 978-1-60320-073-8
ISBN 10: 1-60320-073-8
Library of Congress Control Number:
2009900525

ESSENCE Books is a trademark of Time Inc.

We welcome your comments and
suggestions about ESSENCE Books.
Please write to us at:
ESSENCE Books
Attention: Book Editors
PO Box 11016
Des Moines IA 50336-1016

Front Cover: Photograph by
Gary Hershorn
Back Cover: Photograph by Polaris
Jacket Inset: Photograph by
Pete Souza/The White House/Polaris

If you would like to order any of our
hardcover Collector's Edition books,
please call us at 800-327-6388
(Monday through Friday, 7:00 A.M.–8:00
P.M., or Saturday, 7:00 A.M.–6:00 P.M.
Central Standard Time).

CONTENTS

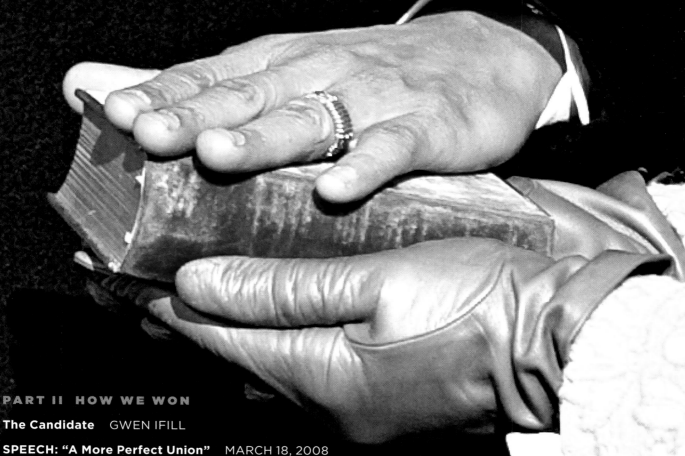

President Obama takes the oath of office with his hand on the Lincoln Bible, held by First Lady Michelle Obama, in Washington, D.C., January 20, 2009.

President Barack Obama and First Lady Michelle Obama greet the enthusiastic crowd who gathered to watch the couple take their first official stroll in the Inaugural Parade in the nation's capital, January 20, 2009.

INTRODUCTION

The election of Barack Obama as the forty-fourth president of the United States is the greatest milestone in our history. This book documents the amazing journey of Barack, his wife Michelle and daughters Malia and Sasha—from the splendidly real Black family they have always been to the first family they have become. ESSENCE was on the sojourn with them from the beginning. We were the first national publication to embrace our now First Lady Michelle Obama, interviewing and photographing her in the summer of 2007.

Throughout the Obamas' journey, ESSENCE editors, writers and photographers captured extraordinary moments for our readers—and not just political moments, but the affectionate glances, visible warmth, caring touches and unabashed love this family showed for one another during the entire challenging campaign. Those times are extra special to us Black Americans. Those pictures are here, along with words from ESSENCE writers, who interviewed and wrote about the Obamas. I trust this celebration will bring you even closer to all they have come to stand for: excellence, determination, faith and family.

For our exclusive September 2008 cover shoot featuring the family, I had an opportunity to walk through their South Side home in Chicago. I watched Malia and Sasha play the piano, and reflected that, like most parents, my greatest wish has been that my own children would inherit a future better than their history. Since that visit, change has come. For my sons, and for every child now and hereafter, the lie of "No, you can't" has been supplanted by the truth of "Yes, we can."

The even larger history lesson that we hope this book carries for us as a people is that we can dust off our broken dreams and redefine what is possible. If a Black man can garner overwhelming interracial support and become president, then we can take hold of other dreams—stable families, safe streets, good schools.

President Obama's historic victory on November 4, 2008, says to every American that our dignity and destiny are in our hands. On behalf of ESSENCE, I hope this book will create everlasting memories of this triumphant moment for you and your loved ones for generations to come.

Angela

Angela Burt-Murray
Editor-in-Chief

"A NEW ERA OF RESPONSIBILITY"

On January 20, 2009, more than 1 million people gathered in the nation's capital to hear Barack Hussein Obama, our forty-fourth and first African-American president, deliver his eagerly anticipated remarks at his historic swearing-in ceremony

My fellow citizens: I stand here today humbled by the task before us, grateful for the trust you have bestowed, mindful of the sacrifices borne by our ancestors. I thank President Bush for his service to our nation, as well as the generosity and cooperation he has shown throughout this transition. Forty-four Americans have now taken the presidential oath. The words have been spoken during rising tides of prosperity and the still waters of peace. Yet, every so often, the oath is taken amidst gathering clouds and raging storms. At these moments, America has carried on not simply because of the skill or vision of those in high office, but because We the People have remained faithful to the ideals of our forebearers, and true to our founding documents. So it has been. So it must be with this generation of Americans.

That we are in the midst of crisis is now well understood. Our nation is at war, against a far-reaching network of violence and hatred. Our economy is badly weakened, a consequence of greed and irresponsibility on the part of some, but also our collective failure to make hard choices and prepare the nation for a new age. Homes have been lost; jobs shed; businesses shuttered. Our health care is too costly; our schools fail too many. And each day brings further evidence that the ways we use energy strengthen our adversaries and threaten our planet.

These are the indicators of crisis, subject to data and statistics. Less measurable but no less profound is a sapping of confidence across our land - a nagging fear that America's decline is inevitable, and that the next generation must lower its sights.

Today I say to you that the challenges we face are real. They are serious and they are many. They will not be met easily or in a short span of time. But know this, America: They will be met.

On this day, we gather because we have chosen hope over fear, unity of purpose over conflict and discord.

On this day, we come to proclaim an end to the petty grievances and false promises, the recriminations and worn-out dogmas, that for far too long have strangled our politics.

We remain a young nation, but in the words of Scripture, the time has come to set aside childish things. The time has come to reaffirm our enduring spirit; to choose our better history; to carry forward that precious gift, that noble idea, passed on from generation to generation: the God-given promise that all are equal, all are free, and all deserve a chance to pursue their full measure of happiness.

In reaffirming the greatness of our nation, we understand that greatness is never a given. It must be earned. Our journey has never been one of shortcuts or settling for less. It has not been the path for the fainthearted - for those who prefer leisure over work, or seek only the pleasures of riches and fame. Rather, it has been the risk takers, the doers, the makers of things - some celebrated, but more often men and women obscure in their labor - who have carried us up the long, rugged path toward prosperity and freedom.

For us, they packed up their few worldly possessions and traveled across oceans in search of a new life.

For us, they toiled in sweatshops and settled the West; endured the lash of the whip and plowed the hard earth.

For us, they fought and died, in places like Concord and Gettysburg; Normandy and Khe Sanh.

Time and again, these men and women struggled and sacrificed and worked till their hands were raw so that we might live a better life. They saw America as bigger than the sum of our individual ambitions; greater than all the differences of birth or wealth or faction.

This is the journey we continue today. We remain the most prosperous, powerful nation on earth. Our workers are no less productive than when this crisis began. Our minds are no less inventive, our goods and services no less needed than they were last week or last month or last year. Our capacity remains undiminished. But our time of standing pat, of protecting narrow interests and putting off unpleasant decisions - that time has surely passed. Starting today, we must pick ourselves up, dust ourselves off, and begin again the work of remaking America.

For everywhere we look, there is work to be done. The state of the economy calls for action, bold and swift, and we will act - not only to create new jobs, but to lay a new foundation for growth. We will build the roads and bridges, the electric grids and digital lines that feed our commerce and bind us together. We will restore science to its rightful place, and wield technology's wonders to raise health care's quality and lower its cost. We will harness the sun and the winds and the soil to fuel our cars and run our factories. And we will transform our schools and colleges and universities to meet the demands of a new age. All this we can do. And all this we will do.

Now, there are some who question the scale of our ambitions

Barack Obama just before he is sworn in as the forty-fourth president of the United States, January 20, 2009.

- who suggest that our system cannot tolerate too many big plans. Their memories are short. For they have forgotten what this country has already done; what free men and women can achieve when imagination is joined to common purpose, and necessity to courage.

What the cynics fail to understand is that the ground has shifted beneath them - that the stale political arguments that have consumed us for so long no longer apply. The question we ask today is not whether our government is too big or too small, but whether it works - whether it helps families find jobs at a decent wage, care they can afford, a retirement that is dignified. Where the answer is yes, we intend to move forward. Where the answer is no, programs will end. And those of us who manage the public's dollars will be held to account - to spend wisely, reform bad

habits, and do our business in the light of day - because only then can we restore the vital trust between a people and their government.

Nor is the question before us whether the market is a force for good or ill. Its power to generate wealth and expand freedom is unmatched. But this crisis has reminded us that without a watchful eye, the market can spin out of control - and that a nation cannot prosper long when it favors only the prosperous. The success of our economy has always depended not just on the size of our gross domestic product, but on the reach of our prosperity; on our ability to extend opportunity to every willing heart - not out of charity, but because it is the surest route to our common good.

As for our common defense, we reject as false the choice between our safety and our ideals. Our Founding Fathers, faced with perils

Massive crowds witness history as Obama becomes the first African-American president of the United States.

we can scarcely imagine, drafted a charter to assure the rule of law and the rights of man, a charter expanded by the blood of generations. Those ideals still light the world, and we will not give them up for expedience's sake. And so to all other peoples and governments who are watching today, from the grandest capitals to the small village where my father was born: Know that America is a friend of each nation and every man, woman and child who seeks a future of peace and dignity, and that we are ready to lead once more.

Recall that earlier generations faced down fascism and communism not just with missiles and tanks, but with sturdy alliances and enduring convictions. They understood that our power alone cannot protect us, nor does it entitle us to do as we please. Instead, they knew that our power grows through its prudent use; our security emanates from the justness of our cause, the force of our example, the tempering qualities of humility and restraint.

We are the keepers of this legacy. Guided by these principles once more, we can meet those new threats that demand even greater effort - even greater cooperation and understanding between nations. We will begin to responsibly leave Iraq to its people, and forge a hard-earned peace in Afghanistan. With old friends and former foes, we will work tirelessly to lessen the nuclear threat, and roll back the specter of a warming planet. We will not apologize for our way of life, nor will we waver in its defense, and for those who seek to advance their aims by inducing terror and slaughtering innocents, we say to you now that our spirit is stronger and cannot be broken; you cannot outlast us, and we will defeat you.

For we know that our patchwork heritage is a strength, not a weakness. We are a nation of Christians and Muslims, Jews and Hindus - and nonbelievers. We are shaped by every language and culture, drawn from every end of this earth. And because we have tasted the bitter swill of civil war and segregation, and emerged from that dark chapter stronger and more united, we cannot help but believe that the old hatreds shall someday pass; that the lines of tribe shall soon dissolve; that as the world grows smaller, our common humanity shall reveal itself; and that America must play its role in ushering in a new era of peace.

To the Muslim world, we seek a new way forward, based on mutual interest and mutual respect. To those leaders around the globe who seek to sow conflict, or blame their society's ills on the West: Know that your people will judge you on what you can build, not what you destroy. To those who cling to power through corruption and deceit and the silencing of dissent, know that you are on the wrong side of history; but that we will extend a hand if you are willing to unclench your fist.

To the people of poor nations, we pledge to work alongside you to make your farms flourish and let clean waters flow; to nourish starved bodies and feed hungry minds. And to those nations like ours that enjoy relative plenty, we say we can no longer afford indifference to suffering outside our borders; nor can we consume the world's resources without regard to effect. For the world has changed, and we must change with it.

As we consider the road that unfolds before us, we remember with humble gratitude those brave Americans who, at this very hour, patrol far-off deserts and distant mountains. They have something to tell us today, just as the fallen heroes who lie in Arlington whisper through the ages. We honor them not only because they are guardians of our liberty, but because they embody the spirit of service; a willingness to find meaning in something greater than themselves. And yet, at this moment - a moment that will define a generation - it is precisely this spirit that must inhabit us all.

For as much as government can do and must do, it is ultimately the faith and determination of the American people upon which this nation relies. It is the kindness to take in a stranger when the levees break, the selflessness of workers who would rather cut their hours than see a friend lose their job which sees us through our darkest hours. It is the firefighter's courage to storm a stairway filled with smoke, but also a parent's willingness to nurture a child, that finally decides our fate.

Our challenges may be new. The instruments with which we meet them may be new. But those values upon which our success depends - honesty and hard work, courage and fair play, tolerance and curiosity, loyalty and patriotism - these things are old. These things are true. They have been the quiet force of progress throughout our history. What is demanded then is a return to these truths. What is required of us now is a new era of responsibility - a recognition, on the part of every American, that we have duties to ourselves, our nation and the world; duties that we do not grudgingly accept but rather seize gladly, firm in the knowledge that there is nothing so satisfying to the spirit, so defining of our character, than giving our all to a difficult task.

This is the price and the promise of citizenship.

This is the source of our confidence - the knowledge that God calls on us to shape an uncertain destiny.

This is the meaning of our liberty and our creed - why men and women and children of every race and every faith can join in celebration across this magnificent mall, and why a man whose father less than 60 years ago might not have been served at a local restaurant can now stand before you to take a most sacred oath.

So let us mark this day with remembrance, of who we are and how far we have traveled. In the year of America's birth, in the coldest of months, a small band of patriots huddled by dying campfires on the shores of an icy river.

The capital was abandoned. The enemy was advancing. The snow was stained with blood. At a moment when the outcome of our revolution was most in doubt, the father of our nation ordered these words be read to the people:

"Let it be told to the future world...that in the depth of winter, when nothing but hope and virtue could survive...that the city and the country, alarmed at one common danger, came forth to meet it."

America, in the face of our common dangers, in this winter of our hardship, let us remember these timeless words. With hope and virtue, let us brave once more the icy currents, and endure what storms may come. Let it be said by our children's children that when we were tested, we refused to let this journey end, that we did not turn back, nor did we falter; and with eyes fixed on the horizon and God's grace upon us, we carried forth that great gift of freedom and delivered it safely to future generations. Thank you. God bless you. And God bless the United States of America.

Part 1

WHO THEY ARE

The Obamas are visible truth of what we've known about our families for some time: We're loving and supportive, ambitious and attentive to one another's needs. When we work hard, strive for excellence, and dream big, everything is possible. No challenge can stop us. We will succeed, together.

President Barack Obama takes the oath as the forty-fourth president of the United States, with his wife, Michelle, by his side. Daughters Malia and Sasha watch, January 20, 2009.

13

THE OBAMAS: PORTRAIT OF AN AMERICAN FAMILY

In a rare interview—and a first for an African-American publication—then Democratic presidential candidate Barack Obama and his family opened up to GWEN IFILL *about their lives, hopes and dreams for each other, our community and our country*

Barack Obama is sitting in the back of his rented luxury campaign bus with its granite counters and two flat-screen TVs. The Illinois senator's arms are wrapped around his wife, Michelle, whom he doesn't get to see much these days. At this very moment he is, of all things, singing.
I've just asked them how their lives have changed since he won the Democratic presidential nomination. There have definitely been changes, especially for Michelle Obama, who used to pride herself on campaigning by day and rushing home to her daughters each night. Now she is spending more of her days and nights on the road, but seldom in the same place as her husband. And when their daughters—Malia, 10, and Sasha, 7—get to see their dad, they likely have to share him with thousands of adoring strangers. "Daddy's gone a lot," Sasha notes. "We don't see him that much."

But on this Fourth of July, everyone is together. Even though there are at least a half-dozen aides and family members on the bus with us, it feels intimate back here. Michelle and Barack are curled up on the beige couch, while the children are reading and coloring a few feet away. Michelle folds her long legs to her chin and leans into her husband as he explains the reality of their lives. When he pauses, she finishes his sentences.

Their ease with each other recalls the day several weeks earlier when Essence arrived to photograph the Obamas at their large Georgian Revival home on Chicago's South Side. Barack stood on the lawn playfully teasing his wife as she posed for our cameras. Now, as then, his customary public caution melts away when he is with his family. Under relentless media scrutiny, Barack Obama says his family is going the extra mile to "maintain this little island of normalcy in the midst of all this swirl of activity." But family snapshots of this sort are rare, as are moments when the Obamas can just chill. "Michelle has done a heroic job of managing the house, the family and still finding time to campaign and be out on the road," he says, after directing staff members to turn off the television, which was tuned to Fox News Channel. "I'm always marveling at everything that she can do."

And then he sings.

"I'm every woman," he croons. She cringes. He laughs. "That's Michelle. It's like, Chaka Khan! Chaka Khan!"

The Michelle Factor

The entire family is on display during a Fourth of July event as

Michelle Obama leads a Montana picnic crowd in a rendition of "Happy Birthday" to daughter Malia, 10. When I ask Malia later exactly how many times she has been sung to that day, she responds with a small smile, "A jillion."

The point is for the Obamas to be together—and have the world watch them doing it. Mom hugs people at the town parade, daughters greet furry parade mascots, Dad flips burgers for hundreds of his newest friends in Big Sky country. Picnickers in Obama for President T-shirts try to catch a glimpse of the candidate, and television cameras are trained on the family's every move.

The frenzy of attention—much of it glaring, some of it negative—never lets up. Aside from the fact that the Obamas could become the nation's first African-American First Couple, there is little new about all this: Presidential candidates and their families have had to cope with such scrutiny almost since the founding of the Republic. People want to know who they are.

But for family members, reading or hearing tough talk about someone you raised can take an adjustment, as Michelle's mother readily admits. "It bothers everyone in the family except Michelle and Barack," says Marian Robinson. "The last time Barack heard us talk about what we heard on the radio, you know what he said?

Sasha (left) and Malia play on a tire swing in Concord, New Hampshire, June 2, 2007.

'Why don't you all stop listening to that?' That's his attitude. When he first said he was going to do this, he said everyone should develop a thick skin, because this is what will happen, and exactly what he said would happen, happened."

For months, Michelle has had to answer for her unfortunately phrased words at a spring campaign event: "For the first time in my adult lifetime, I am really proud of my country," she said, setting off a political firestorm. She insists she was referring to her pride in seeing the level of engagement in this year's political process, but critics have accused her of being insufficiently patriotic. The right-leaning blogosphere, talk show circuit and publishing world rushed to join in: A *National Review* magazine cover featured an angry-looking picture of Michelle with the headline "Mrs. Grievance."

Barack Obama says none of this happens by accident. "There are a group of conservative columnists; they become an echo chamber," he tells ESSENCE. "*The National Review* puts Michelle on the cover, Fox News starts running things in a loop over and over again. They try to create a caricature."

By midsummer, a survey taken by the Associated Press and Yahoo found the "caricature" was winning, with more people viewing Michelle negatively than positively—35 to 30 percent. That's when the Obamas struck back, launching a campaign within a campaign to showcase Michelle as a regular—and nonthreatening—working Mom. Central to that effort was her appearance on ABC's *The View*, where she bumped fists with the cohosts while wearing a $148 sleeveless summer dress that immediately became a retail phenomenon. "You saw what happened when she was on *The View*; she's selling dresses now," Barack says, nudging his wife with a grin. "So I would distinguish between that and the political or the chattering class that very systematically tried to go after her."

Michelle appears unfazed by most of the criticism, focusing instead on what she says she sees as she travels the country—people of all races and descriptions who crowd in to hug her at campaign events, and who do not seem to have gotten the word that she is supposed to be an angry Black woman. "In our generation, we were just taught that if you know who you are, then what somebody calls you is just so irrelevant to the day-to-day issues that have to be a focus of this race," she says, speaking in a rush, as her husband nods in agreement. "If I wilted every time somebody in my life mischaracterized me or called me a bad name, I would have never finished Princeton, would have never gone to Harvard, and wouldn't be sitting here with him. So these are the lessons we want to teach our kids. You know who you are, so whatever anybody else says is just interesting fodder."

Laughing, Michelle's mother acknowledges the advice she gave to her daughter and her son, Craig: "If someone calls you a dog, do you jump down on all fours and start barking? Or do you continue doing whatever you were doing before they called you a dog?"

It's what helps Michelle shrug off the intensity of the campaign. "The values that we've grown up with, that we live and breathe, are pure American values," she reflects. "That is more me than the schools I went to. That is more me than the color of my skin even. That's more me than my gender. I am a mother who wakes up every day worried about the future of her children and the children in our lives. I know how blessed my girls are, because I know too many kids in my family and other communities whose futures are different because of one slip, one mess up, one thing that just didn't work out right. I just know how precarious it is, because I grew up in these communities. But first and foremost," she says, buttoning up her argument, "the reason I think people can connect with me when they see me and get to know me is that I'm just not that different."

Patriot Acts

The Obamas' lives have been transformed by the presence of 24-hour security and lightning-fast media coverage. No detail goes unremarked on, from the precise shade of chartreuse Michelle wears onstage, to the exact blue tone of Barack's tie that he dons for a summertime unity event with Hillary Clinton. On this 90-degree day in the rolling mine country of Butte in southwestern Montana, the Obamas greet supporters as Stevie Wonder's "Signed, Sealed, Delivered (I'm Yours)" wafts from the loudspeakers. In a not-so-subtle response to recurring suggestions that they are just not patriotic enough, the Obamas have chosen to come to Butte on the Fourth of July, the most patriotic of all holidays. The candidate now wears a flag pin on his lapel every day, and Michelle concentrates on proving that, as the product of a working-class Chicago family, she is as mainstream as America gets. In a state where 90 percent of the population is White and only 0.4 percent is Black, the Obamas may well be the largest group of African-Americans the town has recently seen.

Soon enough, the music shifts to Springsteen.

"Montana is a White, blue-collar, rural state," observes Brian Kahn, a White public radio program host who has come to join the event. "I've lived here 20 years and we've never seen anything like this."

This is what they see: Barack's sister, Maya Soetoro-Ng, is the daughter of Obama's Indonesian stepfather and his White mother. Her husband, Konrad, is a Chinese-American born in Canada. Both hold Ph.D.'s and live and work in Honolulu. Their daughter Suhaila laughs and plays with her cousins. Despite the range of ethnicities, as a family, they seem perfectly ordinary. Michelle and her daughters are dressed alike, in sundresses with leggings and flat shoes. Michelle throws a white sweater over her shoulders for photographs, and everyone's hair is pulled back—in Malia's case, in neat cornrows, to guard against the rigors of heat, wind and sudden thunderstorms.

The Obamas pride themselves on creating a family picture that is authentically Black with shades of Norman Rockwell. As Barack stands on a picnic table to talk about health care, energy independence and infrastructure in the blazing high-mountain heat, Malia sits stoically as her mother leans over to press cold bottles of water against her daughter's overheated forehead. By the time Michelle takes the microphone, she is wearing a red, white and blue bolo string tie that Governor Brian Schweitzer has slung around her neck. Michelle La Vaughn Robinson Obama, Ivy League–trained lawyer and well-paid executive, is on hiatus. The supportive wife and working mom has taken her place, singing her husband's praises. Their daughter Malia, confronted on every hand by strangers calling her name, is unfailingly polite to everyone who wants to sing "Happy Birthday" to her or tell her how cute she is, including the governor, and Hartford "Sonny" Black Eagle and his wife, Mary, who were selected by Montana's Crow Indian Nation to be Barack's "adopted grandparents." Sasha generally has a harder time sitting still. She circles around to where her cousin Suhaila sits, plants one, then two kisses on her cheek, then runs back to her mother for permission to strip her feet of her spangly summer sneakers.

Later, there are hula hoops. Someone in the crowd races forward to hand the girls matching pink cowboy hats. This, Barack says, taking in the whole scene, is what America actually looks like, and his campaign is eager to showcase the tableau.

The Good Father

Both Obamas say their travels have convinced them that the racial divide—one of our "national obsessions," Barack calls it—is not as wide or deep as many believe. "I think we don't give the American people enough credit for having undergone a dramatic change, not just in the last 40 years, but even the last 20 years, in terms of racial attitudes," Barack says. "In that sense, my campaign is a testament to how far we've come. I would say that our popular culture still fastens on race the way it fastens on sex, the way it fastens on violence. There's a fascination with it that's not always healthy, and not particularly productive."

Still, the next day it is jarring to leave Butte and fly to St. Louis, where Obama speaks to the Forty-eighth Quadrennial Session of the General Conference of the African Methodist Episcopal Church. The delegates start chanting "Yes, we can!" the moment the candidate steps into view. Aside from the press corps and security, there is nary a White person in sight.

As is often the case when he speaks to an African-American crowd, Obama launches into his stump speech emphasizing the gospel of individual responsibility, sounding for all the world like a cross between Bill Cosby and T.D. Jakes. "I know some people say, 'Why? He's blaming the victim,'" he tells the churchfolks. "I'm not interested in us adopting the posture of victim. I recognize there are outstanding men doing an outstanding job under the most difficult of circumstances. But I also believe that we cannot use injustice as an excuse," he adds, as the congregation cheers. "We can't use poverty as an excuse. There are things within our control that we've got to attend to."

Obama says he has the credibility to speak about sore issues like absent Black fathers, in part, because his father, too, was absent. Barack Obama, Sr., left the family when his son was 2. "It's indisputable that when we've got the majority of African-American children growing up in single-parent households, that that has an impact," he says. "It has an impact, certainly economic. The single biggest indicator of poverty is being a single mom and trying to raise kids. It has an impact socially; it has an impact in terms of how they do in school and their future prospects. Now, there are single moms doing heroic jobs all across America and within the African-American community. And by the way, there are great fathers who are doing the right thing. One of the finest men I ever knew was Michelle's dad, who worked every day despite enormous hardship to make sure his children and his family were cared for."

But, on Father's Day, Obama told the congregation at Apostolic Church of God in Chicago that "we need fathers to realize that responsibility doesn't just end at conception." He went on, "That doesn't just make you a father. What makes you a man is not the ability to have a child. Any fool can have a child. It's the courage to raise a child that makes you a father."

Those comments sparked criticism from many Black Americans, including, notoriously, from the Reverend Jesse Jackson, who used a crude term to express his anger at the candidate for what he described as "talking down" to the Black community. But days before Jackson's comments, in conversations with ESSENCE, Obama had defended his call to responsibility. "The point I was simply trying to make is that you can't keep on using excuses for the failure to be engaged with your child," he says. "Yes, we have a tragic history. Yes, the economy and the collapse of the manufacturing base that used to provide good blue-collar jobs had a disproportionate effect on African-American men. Yes, the problem of drug trade and incarceration rates makes it more difficult for men to stabilize and be there. But there are a lot of middle class men who aren't engaged in their children's lives as well. And I think that's become too culturally acceptable."

The perception among some observers is that there is a campaign calculus that involves Obama making White audiences feel comfortable with him, while doling out straight talk to African-Americans. After two days in Montana, Obama and his entourage swept in and out of St. Louis within two hours, stopping backstage only to receive a blessing from the bishops and preachers. The press was barred.

The Candidate Next Door

Obama's sister, Maya, also grew up largely without her father, and she credits Barack, who is nine years her senior, with filling the gap. She, too, is spending the summer on the campaign trail. Despite the fact that her brother is making history, she says he really hasn't changed much. "He's about the same," she insists. "I mean, honestly, our banter is the same. He's still wonderful in all the same ways, and irritatingly opinionated in all the same ways."

Maya is part of the tight family circle, accompanying her presidential candidate brother to the soccer games and dance recitals he crams in on rare weekends home. Barack's BlackBerry is ever present, his nightly conference calls with campaign staff a constant. But his wife says she gets what she needs.

"The thing that Barack does is that when he is there, he is a parent," says Michelle. "He's not like play dad. He's the guy who has read through all of the Harry Potter books with Malia. Barack is very good about understanding that the kids and their structure and stability are important. And he's somebody who, if there's discipline that needs to be handed down, he doesn't hesitate just because he hasn't seen them in a week."

The Obamas are already seeking advice on how best to protect their girls should they make it to the White House, including where to send them to school. Barack asked Hillary Clinton for her opinion on what worked with Chelsea. Michelle has asked Caroline Kennedy what it was like to be a child of a president, and she plans to call on Tipper Gore. But there is an inevitable absence that is the byproduct of presidential ambition. In the Obama family, the single person most responsible for filling it is Marian Robinson. Michelle's mother lives five minutes away and picks the girls up from school each day to take them to tennis and piano lessons, dance class, soccer practice and play dates. The children are polite and disciplined, playful with other children and respectful with adults. They get that from their mother, who got it from her mother.

It was Robinson's idea, for instance, that the girls not receive gifts for their birthdays. Instead, each is allowed to choose something she would like to do, instead of what she would like to get. "It's more important for them to be exposed and be active," Robinson says in a telephone conversation.

This does not mean Grandma doesn't sneak them the occasional ice cream treat. She does. And if helping Michelle means she might have to move to Washington, D.C., she'll do that too.

For now, living on Chicago's Black South Side, where the family

The Obamas at the Iowa State Fair in August 2007.

resides in a gated $1.65 million Hyde Park home that is only a stone's throw from what Michelle freely describes as "the 'hood," has kept them aware of the problems plaguing African-Americans such as diabetes, HIV/AIDS and breast cancer. When I mention that I haven't heard AIDS—which has reached crisis status among Black women—come up much in the campaign, Barack agrees that it's a critical issue he has talked about and should talk about. "There is no illness that we are not disproportionately affected by," he says. Michelle picks up the thought: "A lot of us don't have access to primary preventive health care. People can't afford regular doctors."

Michelle says their home turf keeps them grounded in other ways as well. "One of the things I like best about this, what we're doing, is that we still live on the South Side," she says. "So for all of this wonderful madness that comes along with our lives—the Secret Service, the cars—there are kids on Forty-seventh and King Drive who can walk two blocks and be that close for the first time to somebody who can be the president of the United States.

I love that... I like for them to be able to walk and stand in front of our house and see him up close and personal. 'This man lives in my neighborhood.'"

"They don't know where Kennebunkport is," Barack adds, referring to the Bush family compound in Maine, "but they know where the South Side is."

He recalls one of the most powerful moments on the campaign trail. "A White woman comes up to me and says, 'My son teaches in an inner-city school in San Francisco, and he's told me that during the course of your campaign he's noticed that the Black boys in the class are working harder, are more focused, are fascinated by this whole thing,'" he says. "You know kids just want to feel like they've got a shot. If they can recognize something that gives them some sense of a path to achievement and respect, they absorb it like sponges."

Trying for Normal

Despite all that has changed for them publicly, the Obamas insist that little has changed in their private lives. Their friends are the same. And the family treats them the same, as at their last Thanksgiving. "Everybody came over to our house just like nobody was running for president," Michelle says, laughing.

And sometimes the Obamas find ways to merge their two lives. At the end of the day in Butte, Montana, the family returned to the local Holiday Inn Express where they were staying, ordered dinner in from a local restaurant, ate cake, and cranked up birthday girl Malia's favorite music: Beyoncé, the Jonas Brothers and Hannah Montana. "We just spent about two hours dancing and singing, rocking out," Barack told the reporters on his campaign plane the next day. "Malia said it was the best birthday she'd ever had." He pauses, then adds wistfully: "I don't know if she was just telling us what we wanted to hear, but I can tell you from my perspective, it was one of the best times I have had in a long time."

This article first appeared in the September 2008 issue of ESSENCE.

JASON REED/REUTERS/LANDOV

The Obamas teach their
daughters to skate
in Lafayette, Indiana,
May 3, 2008.

"A NEW BIRTH OF FREEDOM"

On February 10, 2007, Democratic Senator Barack Obama of Illinois announced his candidacy for president in Springfield, Illinois, where Abraham Lincoln once served. Obama delivered an uplifting message of hope before more than 15,000 people

Let me begin by saying thanks to all of you who've traveled, from far and wide, to brave the cold today. We all made this journey for a reason. It's humbling, but in my heart I know you didn't come here just for me, you came here because you believe in what this country can be. In the face of war, you believe there can be peace. In the face of despair, you believe there can be hope. In the face of a politics that's shut you out, that's told you to settle, that's divided us for too long, you believe we can be one people, reaching for what's possible, building that more perfect union.

That's the journey we're on today. But let me tell you how I came to be here. As most of you know, I am not a native of this great state. I moved to Illinois over two decades ago. I was a young man then, just a year out of college; I knew no one in Chicago, was without money or family connections. But a group of churches had offered me a job as a community organizer for $13,000 a year. And I accepted the job, sight unseen, motivated then by a single, simple, powerful idea - that I might play a small part in building a better America.

My work took me to some of Chicago's poorest neighborhoods. I joined with pastors and laypeople to deal with communities that had been ravaged by plant closings. I saw that the problems people faced weren't simply local in nature - that the decision to close a steel mill was made by distant executives; that the lack of textbooks and computers in schools could be traced to the skewed priorities of politicians a thousand miles away; and that when a child turns to violence, there's a hole in his heart no government alone can fill.

It was in these neighborhoods that I received the best education I ever had, and where I learned the true meaning of my Christian faith.

After three years of this work, I went to law school, because I wanted to understand how the law should work for those in need. I became a civil rights lawyer, and taught constitutional law, and after a time, I came to understand that our cherished rights of liberty and equality depend on the active participation of an awakened electorate. It was with these ideas in mind that I arrived in this capital city as a state senator.

It was here, in Springfield, where I saw all that is America converge - farmers and teachers, businessmen and laborers, all of them with a story to tell, all of them seeking a seat at the table, all of them clamoring to be heard. I made lasting friendships here - friends that I see in the audience today.

It was here we learned to disagree without being disagreeable - that it's possible to compromise so long as you know those principles that can never be compromised; and that so long as we're willing to listen to each other, we can assume the best in people instead of the worst.

That's why we were able to reform a death penalty system that was broken. That's why we were able to give health insurance to children in need. That's why we made the tax system more fair and just for working families, and that's why we passed ethics reforms that the cynics said could never, ever be passed.

It was here in Springfield, where North, South, East and West come together, that I was reminded of the essential decency of the American people - where I came to believe that through this decency, we can build a more hopeful America.

And that is why, in the shadow of the Old State Capitol, where Lincoln once called on a divided house to stand together, where common hopes and common dreams still live, I stand before you today to announce my candidacy for president of the United States.

I recognize there is a certain presumptuousness - a certain audacity - to this announcement. I know I haven't spent a lot of time learning the ways of Washington. But I've been there long enough to know that the ways of Washington must change.

The genius of our founders is that they designed a system of government that can be changed. And we should take heart, because we've changed this country before. In the face of tyranny, a band of patriots brought an empire to its knees. In the face of secession, we unified a nation and set the captives free. In the face of depression, we put people back to work and lifted millions out of poverty. We welcomed immigrants to our shores, we opened railroads to the West, we landed a man on the moon, and we heard a King's call to let justice roll down like water, and righteousness like a mighty stream.

Each and every time, a new generation has risen up and done what's needed to be done. Today we are called once more - and it is time for our generation to answer that call.

For that is our unyielding faith - that in the face of impossible odds, people who love their country can change it.

That's what Abraham Lincoln understood. He had his doubts. He had his defeats. He had his setbacks. But through his will and his words, he moved a nation and helped free a people. It is because of the millions who rallied to his cause that we are no longer divided, North and South, slave and free. It is because men and women of every race, from every

Senator Barack Obama (D-IL) formally announces his campaign for U.S. president in the 2008 election during a rally in Springfield, Illinois, February 10, 2007.

walk of life, continued to march for freedom long after Lincoln was laid to rest, that today we have the chance to face the challenges of this millennium together, as one people - as Americans.

All of us know what those challenges are today - a war with no end, a dependence on oil that threatens our future, schools where too many children aren't learning, and families struggling paycheck to paycheck despite working as hard as they can. We know the challenges. We've heard them. We've talked about them for years.

What's stopped us from meeting these challenges is not the absence of sound policies and sensible plans. What's stopped us is the failure of leadership, the smallness of our politics - the ease with which we're distracted by the petty and trivial, our chronic avoidance of tough decisions, our preference for scoring cheap political points instead of rolling up our sleeves and building a working consensus to tackle big problems.

For the last six years we've been told that our mounting debts don't matter, we've been told that the anxiety Americans feel about rising health care costs and stagnant wages are an illusion, we've been told that climate change is a hoax, and that tough talk and an ill-conceived war can replace diplomacy, and strategy, and foresight. And when all else fails, when Katrina happens, or the death toll in Iraq mounts, we've been told that our crises are somebody else's fault. We're distracted from our real failures, and told to blame the other party, or gay people, or immigrants.

And as people have looked away in disillusionment and frustration, we know what's filled the void. The cynics, and the lobbyists, and the special interests who've turned our government into a game only they can afford to play. They write the checks and you get stuck with the bills, they get the access while you get to write a letter, they think they own this government, but we're here today to take it back. The time for that politics is over. It's time to turn the page.

We've made some progress already. I was proud to help lead the fight in Congress that led to the most sweeping ethics reform since Watergate.

But Washington has a long way to go. And it won't be easy. That's why we'll have to set priorities. We'll have to make hard choices. And although government will play a crucial role in bringing about the changes we need, more money and programs alone will not get us

Obama and his wife, Michelle, greet supporters from the stage after he announced his candidacy for U.S. president.

where we need to go. Each of us, in our own lives, will have to accept responsibility - for instilling an ethic of achievement in our children, for adapting to a more competitive economy, for strengthening our communities, and sharing some measure of sacrifice. So let us begin. Let us begin this hard work together. Let us transform this nation.

Let us be the generation that reshapes our economy to compete in the digital age. Let's set high standards for our schools and give them the resources they need to succeed. Let's recruit a new army of teachers, and give them better pay and more support in exchange for more accountability. Let's make college more affordable, and let's invest in scientific research, and let's lay down broadband lines through the heart of inner cities and rural towns all across America.

And as our economy changes, let's be the generation that ensures our nation's workers are sharing in our prosperity. Let's protect the hard-earned benefits their companies have promised. Let's make it possible for hardworking Americans to save for retirement. And let's allow our unions and their organizers to lift up this country's middle class again.

Let's be the generation that ends poverty in America. Every single person willing to work should be able to get job training that leads to a job, and earn a living wage that can pay the bills, and afford child care so their kids have a safe place to go when they work. Let's do this.

Let's be the generation that finally tackles our health care crisis. We can control costs by focusing on prevention, by providing better treatment to the chronically ill, and using technology to cut the bureaucracy. Let's be the generation that says right here, right now, that we will have universal health care in America by the end of the next president's first term.

Let's be the generation that finally frees America from the tyranny of oil. We can harness homegrown, alternative fuels like ethanol and spur the production of more fuel-efficient cars. We can set up a system for capping greenhouse gases. We can turn this crisis of global warming into a moment of opportunity for innovation, and job creation, and an incentive for businesses that will serve as a model for the world. Let's be the generation that makes future generations proud of what we did here.

Most of all, let's be the generation that never forgets what happened on that September day and confront the terrorists with everything we've got. Politics doesn't have to divide us on this anymore - we can work together to keep our country safe. I've worked with Republican Senator Dick Lugar to pass a law that will secure and destroy some of the world's deadliest, unguarded weapons. We can work together to track terrorists down with a stronger military, we can tighten the net around their finances, and we can improve our intelligence capabilities. But let us also understand that ultimate victory against our enemies will come only by rebuilding our alliances and exporting those ideals that bring hope and opportunity to millions around the globe.

But all of this cannot come to pass until we bring an end to this war in Iraq. Most of you know I opposed this war from the start. I thought it was a tragic mistake. Today we grieve for the families who have lost loved ones, the hearts that have been broken, and the young lives that could have been. America, it's time to start bringing our troops home. It's time to admit that no amount of American lives can resolve the political disagreement that lies at the heart of someone else's civil war. That's why I have a plan that will bring our combat troops home by March of 2008. Letting the Iraqis know that we will not be there forever is our last, best hope to pressure the Sunni and Shia to come to the table and find peace.

Finally, there is one other thing that is not too late to get right about this war - and that is the homecoming of the men and women - our veterans - who have sacrificed the most. Let us honor their valor by providing the care they need and rebuilding the military they love. Let us be the generation that begins this work.

I know there are those who don't believe we can do all these things. I understand the skepticism. After all, every four years, candidates from both parties make similar promises, and I expect this year will be no different. All of us running for president will travel around the country offering ten-point plans and making grand speeches; all of us will trumpet those qualities we believe make us uniquely qualified to lead the country.

But too many times, after the election is over, and the confetti is swept away, all those promises fade from memory, and the lobbyists and the special interests move in, and people turn away, disappointed as before, left to struggle on their own.

That is why this campaign can't only be about me.

It must be about us - it must be about what we can do together. This campaign must be the occasion, the vehicle, of your hopes, and your dreams. It will take your time, your energy, and your advice - to push us forward when we're doing right, and to let us know when we're not. This campaign has to be about reclaiming the meaning of citizenship, restoring our sense of common purpose, and realizing that few obstacles can withstand the power of millions of voices calling for change.

By ourselves, this change will not happen. Divided, we are bound to fail. But the life of a tall, gangly, self-made Springfield lawyer tells us that a different future is possible.

He tells us that there is power in words.

He tells us that there is power in conviction.

That beneath all the differences of race and region, faith and station, we are one people.

He tells us that there is power in hope.

As Lincoln organized the forces arrayed against slavery, he was heard to say: "Of strange, discordant, and even hostile elements, we gathered from the four winds, and formed and fought to battle through."

That is our purpose here today.

That's why I'm in this race.

Not just to hold an office, but to gather with you to transform a nation. I want to win that next battle - for justice and opportunity.

I want to win that next battle - for better schools, and better jobs, and health care for all.

I want us to take up the unfinished business of perfecting our union, and building a better America.

And if you will join me in this improbable quest, if you feel destiny calling, and see as I see, a future of endless possibility stretching before us; if you sense, as I sense, that the time is now to shake off our slumber, and slough off our fear, and make good on the debt we owe past and future generations, then I'm ready to take up the cause, and march with you, and work with you.

Together, starting today, let us finish the work that needs to be done, and usher in a new birth of freedom on this earth.

President Barack Obama and First Lady Michelle Obama dance on a replica of the presidential seal at the Commander in Chief's Ball in Washington, D.C., January 20, 2009.

BESIDE BARACK

As her husband's political star ascended and the race for the White House heated up, Michelle Obama, *an accomplished woman in her own right, kept Barack Obama grounded and her finger on the pulse of what women were thinking.* Journalist GWEN IFILL *joined her on the campaign trail*

Michelle Obama strolls through the campaign headquarters on the eleventh floor of a nondescript downtown Chicago high-rise like a queen. Long-limbed and striking, she is not dressed like a candidate's wife. No jewel-toned knits or demure knee-length skirts. It's hot outside, so her shoulders are bare. Campaign workers fall silent as she glides by, more awed than intimidated.

Michelle Obama, wife of Illinois Senator Barack Obama, does not act like a candidate's wife, either. When standing on stage by her husband's side, there is none of that dutiful head nodding. Her gaze is fixed on him but there is not an ounce of subservience in it. Still it is clear that when they are together he is the person commanding the stage.

But as her husband continues to turn heads in his bid to become the nation's first African-American president, Michelle Obama just might be the campaign's secret weapon.

On the Road With Michelle

It is the early days of this campaign, so covering Michelle Obama is not yet the mob experience it soon will be. This is my sixth presidential campaign, and it feels downright peaceful. Part of this comes from traveling with the spouse, not the principal. The other part comes from being in the presence of Michelle Obama herself. In years of watching candidates negotiate long campaign days, I've seen a lot of them sweat. Not Michelle. Cool and certain, she makes it clear that she has embarked on this adventure on her own terms.

When campaigning solo, as she was at an awards luncheon in New York City recently, Michelle is apt to scribble her own remarks, and then toss them aside if the occasion warrants it. That sort of flexibility comes in handy when the lawyer you married decides he wants to be president of the United States. Her role is key to the plan to pull this

Michelle at her home in
Chicago, June 19, 2008.

off, because with the loyalties of women voters in the balance, the hope is that Michelle will help Barack tip the scales. On the stump, her studied warmth is a contrast to her husband's brainy cool. More than one person in the Obama camp whispers that she, in fact, is the more compelling speaker.

"We need to change the face of the conversation, ladies," she tells the mostly female audience at a rally in Las Vegas. "We sat back too long, suffering in silence, avoiding these challenges. We can't do that any longer. We need a man"—she stops and edits herself—"a person who happens to be a man, who is ready to help us turn the page to bring a new conversation to the table, to change the lives of women and children across America."

I first encountered the Obamas in the most public of ways: onstage at the 2004 Democratic National Convention, minutes after he had completed a raucously received speech about hope and unity. With the sheen of the moment still bouncing off them both, they waded through the applause over to my NewsHour camera position. I asked him one of those awful broadcaster's questions: How did it feel?

"You're just trying to make sure you don't screw up," he responded.

It wasn't until two years later, in his best-selling book, *The Audacity of Hope*, that I discovered where those words came from: Michelle. Her final words to him before he went to the podium that night—delivered with a hug —were, "Just don't screw it up, buddy."

Since then, Michelle has been both admired and criticized for being a successful working mother who decided to take a backseat to her husband's ambitions. But she is not listening to the critics. "I know who I need to be," she tells me as she cools her heels in a borrowed conference room between campaign appearances in New York. "I've come to know myself at the age of 43. Now maybe if I were 23 or 33, I'd still be struggling with that. But I'm a grown-up. And I've seen it up, and I've seen it down, and I know who I need to be to stay true to who I am and to keep my family on track. We don't always figure that out for ourselves as women."

Barack Obama, chatting by phone from the trail, says, "There's no doubt that a lot of women identify with Michelle, because she's prototypical of women who came of age when they had career opportunities that didn't exist in the past, yet they continue to cherish and value their family lives." Still, Michelle admits it's not easy.

"I think my generation of professional women are sort of waking up and realizing that we potentially may not be able to have it all—not at the same time," she says.

From the South Side to Princeton

As the nation figures out who Michelle Obama is, she could well end up being this year's big Rorschach test. How will Americans react to an educated Black woman who adheres to no widely accepted stereotype?

Nettie Harrison, a retired Black educator who braved the heat to see Michelle in Las Vegas, says she expected to hear more about the political than the personal, but was pleased it was the other way around. "So many times we have people who are born with that spoon in their mouth," she says, as Michelle shook hands a few feet away, "and they have no concept of where a lot of us have come from, or where we are going."

Where Michelle LaVaughn Robinson "came from" is the storied South Side of Chicago. She grew up with her older brother, Craig, in a modest bungalow owned by working-class parents. Their father, Fraser Robinson, who died in 1990, worked as a pump operator most of his adult life. Even though he suffered from multiple sclerosis, he managed to send his children to Princeton and leave a pension for his widow.

Craig is now a men's basketball coach at Brown University in Providence. "What you see when you see my sister is my sister," he tells ESSENCE. "You don't see someone pretending to be someone else or someone who thought she was going to grow up to be a first lady."

After graduating from Princeton with honors in 1985, Michelle earned a Harvard law degree in 1988, and went home to work in the law firm of Sidley Austin Brown & Wood, where she met Barack. She was initially assigned to supervise her future husband.

"I thought, *This is probably just a Black man who can talk straight. That's why they're excited about him*," she tells audiences. So she lowered her expectations. But he was cuter than she expected. And Barack took her to church basements, where he spoke to groups of inner-city women who were more worried about making the rent than marching on City Hall. "He connected with me and everyone in that church basement, just like he is connecting with you," she tells the women in Las Vegas. "He was able to articulate a vision that resonated with people, that was real. And right then and there, I decided this guy was special. The authenticity you see is real, and that's why I fell in love with him."

Michelle Obama's career since then has been a blend of public service and public and private practice. Her experience, she says, influences her latest risky role: stepping out onto the political ledge to grasp for an elusive brass ring. There is a chance they might slip, a chance they might fall, but in her down-to-earth way, Michelle says it's a risk they will take. "Our challenges get publicized, and I see that as a gift to let people know there is no magic to this," she says. But observers want to know: What kind of first lady would Michelle Obama be? The Hillary Clinton model—a power behind the throne? Or the Laura Bush model—a demure partner who does actually invite people to the White House for tea?

Whatever it takes, she says. "If that means that the country needs a more traditional first lady, well, I can do that. It would not emasculate me," she says, leaning forward in the Chicago conference room. "But it wouldn't look like everybody else's; it would have a Michelle Obama flair to it, right? Because I am who I am."

Still Grounded

Michelle likes to remind audiences her husband is just a man—at once extraordinary and quite ordinary—a man who forgets to pick up his socks. Her intent is to humanize the man many see as the Great Black Hope. She is untroubled by early critics who have said she is too dismissive of her husband, or that she should not have scaled back her career to serve his presidential ambitions. "I know that I can't do it all," she offers flatly as we chat in Chicago. "I cannot be involved in a presidential campaign, hold down a full-time senior-level position, get my kids to camp, and exercise and eat right. I know I can't do it all. So forgive me for being human, but I'm going to put it on the table. You've got to make trade-offs in life. I'm okay with that. I've come to realize I am sacrificing one set of things in my life for something else potentially really positive."

That "something" is the vision of her husband in the White House as the nation's first African-American president. If that sounds audacious, that's because it is. And in her own way—she works out every morning and tells her audiences they should too, she's raising two girls while running a major health-care system, and her nails and hair are never unkempt—Michelle Obama is audacious, too. But, just as an assertive woman is so frequently labeled aggressive, an audacious Black woman runs the risk of appearing—well, there is not another way to say it—uppity. In the political world, where the spotlight shines especially bright, perception is everything. So there is no talk in the Obama campaign of a "two-for-one" presidency, as there was when Bill and Hillary Clinton ran in 1992. And Senator Obama says he doubts his wife would even want a White House policy gig. "That tends not to be the role Michelle likes to play," he says. "She knows she's got influence with me and doesn't need to be overt to let her opinions get known."

A few weeks after meeting in New York City, we are in Las Vegas, where it is 100 degrees outside. A couple of hundred women have crowded into a community center to see Michelle. She looks as fresh as ever, but this is not her normal comfort zone. She has stepped back from her $213,000 salary as vice-president of community and external affairs for the University of Chicago Hospitals to step up to the unpredictability of the trail.

"I'm here not just because I'm the wife of a candidate," she tells the attentive audience, most of them middle-aged women, many of them Black. "Because this is hard," she says with a hint of weariness in her voice. "This is really a hard thing. This isn't a natural choice to be made in your life. It's strange, all this."

So why bother?

"I'm here as a woman, as a mother, as a citizen of this country," she goes on, smiling as she connects to the crowd. "And I am so tired of the way things are." When Michelle speaks like this, a little of the South Side comes out. She has a matter-of-fact delivery that is familiar to Black women—less so to others.

While her husband's campaign may have been embraced by many convinced he can somehow "transcend race," one of those people is not his wife. While in New York City, we walk past a television tuned to CNN. Barack Obama, the newscaster reports, is about to become the first candidate in the race—other than Hillary Clinton—to get Secret Service protection.

When I visit with her at the campaign's Chicago headquarters weeks later, I ask if any of this scares her. "Something might happen," she concedes. "But you know what? Something really powerful might also happen. And you might grow and learn and benefit others."

Older African-Americans worry about Barack's safety, but she says we must let go of fear. "We've let fear squash us for real legitimate reasons," she says. "But if you focus on fear, you do nothing."

Senator Obama acknowledges his wife was resistant at first to the idea of his running for president two years into his first Senate term. "We haven't had a lot of peace and quiet over the last four years,"

he says. "Michelle's always had veto power, and always will, over decisions that have a direct impact on her."

David Axelrod, the campaign's chief strategist, says Michelle's veto power played out in the weeks leading up to the campaign. "She was interested in whether it was a crazy, harebrained idea," he says over coffee in Chicago. "Because she's not into crazy, harebrained ideas."

Ultimately, Michelle concluded Barack had to go for it. And so did she. "I took myself down every dark road you could go on, just to prepare myself before we jumped out there," she says. *"Are we emotionally, financially ready for this?* I dreamed out all the scenarios. The bottom line is, man, the little sacrifice we have to make is nothing compared to the possibility of what we could do if this catches on."

For Michelle, the campaign is a particularly intricate juggling act. In Las Vegas, she began her day scarfing down a veggie frittata at a breakfast for selected supporters. Her daughters, Malia, 9, and Sasha, 6,

Michelle and her mother, Marian Robinson, share a laugh at the Democratic National Convention, August 26, 2008.

were back in the hotel playing with the remote control and preparing for an afternoon at the pool.

The girls, and sometimes Michelle's mother, Marian Robinson, travel with her when they are not attending private school in Chicago. Back home, she explains, "I've got my community, family, neighbors, girlfriends, my parents, people who have known us forever. And it's easier to stay grounded if the people you are surrounding yourself with really know you. You can't get too big or too taken if your mother's looking at you thinking, *I know who you are.*"

A Method to the Madness

As the campaign has come to demand more and more of her time, it's fallen to Michelle to hit the trail by day and be mother by night. That is a big part of the story she tells on the stump.

"I get them to a neighbor's if I can't get them to school," she says of her children, as women in the audience nod. "I get on a plane. I come to a city. I do several events. I get on a plane. I get home before bedtime. And by doing that, yeah, I'm a little tired at the end of the day, but the girls, they just think Mommy was at work. They don't know I was in New Hampshire. Quite frankly, they don't care."

The Obamas could not possibly have any idea what awaits them. The white-hot spotlight of 1600 Pennsylvania Avenue is like no other. Everything, from how she dresses and where they choose to send the kids to school, will become fodder for every pundit and blogger with a laptop. Her solution? Put other people's outsized expectations aside, and take it as it comes. "I tell myself all the time, we're supposed to take the risk," she says. "In the end, I think we have an obligation to give it a shot. To do our best. To give people a choice."

This article first appeared in the September 2007 issue of ESSENCE.

Michelle waves at the end of her triumphant speech at the Democratic National Convention in Denver, August 25, 2008.

Wife and daughters enjoy listening to their presidential favorite as he speaks during an early campaign stop in Oskaloosa, Iowa, July 4, 2007.

35

THE POSSIBLE DREAM

The Obama campaign resonated unlike any other in our history, especially with young people. Now children from this day forward will not recall a time when there wasn't a Black president of the United States of America
By Marian Wright Edelman

A cartoon in the 1960's showed a Black boy saying to a White boy: "I'll sell you my chance to be president of the United States for a nickel." President Obama was then a toddler, and the overwhelming majority of Black southerners were denied the right to vote. That little boy's chances—and yours—changed dramatically on November 4, 2008. I was deeply moved that enough Americans of all colors would be willing to do for you and for all of our nation's and world's children what Dr. King dreamed—vote for a president based on the content of his character and intellect rather than the color of his skin.

I am so proud of America. I am so proud of the Obama family, whose image and accomplishments will change stereotypes about Black families and what Black people can accomplish. Always remember this miraculous moment in our nation's history, the result of so many decades of Black struggle and sacrifice. And please remember our new leader's example and lessons: Your color has nothing to do with your worth. You are as good as anyone, depending on what is in your heart and head. Set a goal, persevere, stay in school, study hard, and let no obstacle deter you. The impossible is possible with vision, character, discipline, hard work and a "Yes, We Can" attitude.

This election, in which young people played such a big role, says to every child of color that you belong, too; you can be and do anything any child can; and you can make a difference no matter how poor you are, what family type you have or what hue your skin is. So hold on to your dreams and never let anyone tell you your young voice doesn't count. You can change the world—and did.

This article first appeared in the January 2009 issue of ESSENCE.

Obama kisses 5-month-old Daryn Bailey Binns after speaking to supporters in Columbia, South Carolina, on January 20, 2008, as he campaigns for the state's Democratic primary.

Michelle and the girls escape a summer shower at a campaign rally in Butte, Montana, July 4, 2008.

Malia and Sasha at a house party in Hanover, New Hampshire, May 28, 2007.

41

NGE

BAMA.COM

Barack and Michelle
have a moment
together after a
successful rally in
Miami, Florida,
October 21, 2008.

PART 2
HOW WE WON

By being down-to-earth and grounded in faith, by embracing new ideas and encouraging us to cope with change, the Obamas never lost their cool. They invited everyone to reinvest in our nation's future, from the millions who donated, sometimes as little as $5, to the thousands of willing workers, young and young at heart, who knocked on doors, raised funds and consciousness, sent text messages and e-mails, and spread the word about the visionary man who is now the leader of the free world.

Obama shares a laugh with supporters on the campus of Atlanta's Georgia Tech in April 2007 as he sought the Democratic nomination for president. An estimated 20,000 people attended his campaign rally.

Barack Obama accepts the nomination for president at the Democratic National Convention before nearly 80,000 people at Invesco Stadium in Denver, August 28, 2008.

During the campaign's final days, Obama is cheered by a crowd of more than 100,000 people in Denver, October 26, 2008.

49

Obama connects with Lester L. Jones, Sr., and his customers in Jones's Fort Lauderdale, Florida, salon, October 21, 2008.

An essential must-have on the campaign trail: a bowl of gumbo with hot sauce at Dookie Chase's Restaurant, where owner Leah Chase is Obama's host, in New Orleans, February 7, 2008.

Obama is engulfed during a rally at the Xcel Energy Center in St. Paul, June 3, 2008. He had just clinched the Democratic presidential nomination following that day's primaries in South Dakota and Montana, although Hillary Clinton had not yet conceded the race.

Obama rests on the campaign bus, driving from Hanover to Nashua, the morning of the New Hampshire primary, January 8, 2008.

THE CANDIDATE

*With a fund-raising machine in overdrive, a rock-star image, a message of unity
and inclusion, and powerful friends like Oprah Winfrey,
Illinois Senator Barack Obama continued his bid to become America's first Black president.
Journalist* GWEN IFILL *joined him on the campaign trail*

Barack Obama is telling me a story about his 9-year-old daughter, Malia. They were walking to the bookstore on a rare weekend home in Chicago, being followed at a distance by strapping men in dark glasses and earpieces—the Secret Service entourage that has shadowed the Illinois senator since May. The "secret people" Malia and her 6-year-old sister, Sasha, call them. "Malia asked, 'Have you always wanted to run for president?'" he recalls with a half smile. "I said, 'No, not really; it's something that I kind of grew into.'" Then he posed his own question: "'What do you think? Do you think you'd want to be president?'" he remembers asking. Her response: "No, not really. The problem with being president is, if you say something, it's always a big deal. If you're an actress and you say the wrong line in a play, that's sort of the end of it. If you're president and you say something wrong, it could be a really big mess. That's too much pressure." Recalling the conversation, Obama smiles, as if this is the kind of father–daughter chat every family has. In fact, it is nothing short of astonishing that any Black parent can tell such a story at all. At a time when we worry about the state of the Black family in America, and the nature of politics, here is a Black man chatting with his daughter about being president. And though Malia is correct about the pressure, so far, her dad seems up to it. I've never really seen Barack Obama sweat. Not when I first met him right after he delivered his star turn 2004 Democratic National Convention keynote speech. Not during debates when front-runner Hillary Clinton took him on. And not this summer when he coolly told a convention of Black journalists who had been debating whether he is "Black enough" that they should concern themselves with weightier things. "I want to apologize for being a little bit late," he riffs as he arrives onstage at the National Association of Black Journalists (NABJ) Convention in Las Vegas. "But you guys keep asking whether I'm Black enough." A pause while laughter builds. "So I figured I'd stroll in."

It was an inside joke that mystified Whites in the room, but the Black journalists convulsed with laughter. The truth is, Obama is seldom late, but now, when he could be a mere few months away from besting one of the nation's top politicians at her own game—or watching his campaign crumble in a defeated heap in Iowa or New Hampshire—coolness counts. Obama handles the pressure on some days better than on others. He has sustained his share of political attacks this campaign season as he mounted a newcomer's challenge strong enough to draw fire from both Democrats and Republicans. But this is one of the good days. Flying into a small airport in New Hampshire's Lakes Region, Obama has attracted a crowd, as usual. Today, in tiny Laconia, it is only a couple hundred, but it is a Monday afternoon. And, because first impressions count and the Granite State's primary is the nation's first, crowds—regardless of their size—matter in make-or-break New Hampshire. Bounding through the throng with a lanky ease, the junior senator from Illinois smiles broadly, kisses babies and basks in the praise of adoring strangers. "Everywhere we go we've been seeing these terrific crowds," he exults to the lunchtime onlookers, pushing his voice past the limitations of a mild head cold. "Twenty thousand people show up in Atlanta. Twenty thousand people in Austin, Texas. We had 15,000 in Oakland.

"People have asked me what accounts for all this," he continues. "I would love to take all the credit myself and say it's because I'm just so terrific. But I have to say it's not about me. The reason people are coming out is they are burning with a want and a desire for change."

Betty O'Neill, an 85-year-old White woman with white cotton candy hair, is one of them. She's sitting on a bench at the diner across the street with her husband, Stan. "Everybody, this is our next president," she exclaims as Obama strides over to shake her hand and favor her with his trademark toothy smile. She is still grinning and nudging her husband as he moves on. But here, as almost everywhere, Hillary Clinton, who has been campaigning in New Hampshire for herself or her husband for 15 years, has beaten him to the punch. The first thing Obama encounters inside the diner is a smiling picture of his rival posing with the waitresses, taken when she dropped by two weeks before. Unfazed, Obama, in shirtsleeves with a BlackBerry strapped to his belt and photographers trailing behind, works the room. And he poses for his picture too.

More than a dozen other Democrats and Republicans have spent the better part of the year pounding the turf in New Hampshire, Iowa, South Carolina and Nevada and a half-dozen other states. They, too, say they are the formula for change. But Obama is the newest one on the stage. Just two years out of the Illinois State Senate and born in 1961, he is the youngest candidate in either party. If he were to become president, his would certainly be the most unconventional road ever taken to the White House. Born in Hawaii to a Black father from Kenya who left when Obama was 2, and a White mother from Kansas, he was raised in large part by his White grandparents.

In his best-selling 1995 memoir, *Dreams From My Father*, Obama revealed he gave far more thought to this duality than most of us ever have to. "I ceased to advertise my mother's race at the age of 12 or 13, when I suspected that by doing so I was ingratiating myself to Whites," he writes. Now, winning this election means he will have to ingratiate

CALLIE SHELL/AURORA

Boarding his plane before a flight to Sarasota, Florida, October 30, 2008.

himself to Whites, Blacks and every shade and ethnicity in between.

High voter engagement, especially in the critical early states, suggests that everyone is taking stock. National surveys showed Clinton in the lead, while polls in the key states showed Obama mounting a stiff challenge. Is the difference due to familiarity or to race? It's hard to tell. While Obama's biracial background may be appealing to some Whites because he seems less Black, he could be rejected by some Blacks because he seems too White.

"I think in part we're still locked in this notion that somehow if you appeal to White folks there must be something wrong," Obama tells the packed audience of Black journalists.

Georgetown University professor Michael Eric Dyson calls Obama's dilemma the "pigment predicate." "At this level, race is trumping gender when it comes to the discomfort his candidacy might ultimately cause in the American citizenry," Dyson reflects. "And I think Barack Obama is caught in the crosswinds of race."

Obama acknowledges the tightrope he walks. "What I've tried to do is just to say what I think and not worry about whether it's pleasing a particular audience or not," he says, slouched slightly in a chair after a lunchtime campaign appearance. "It is difficult because what I say oftentimes is read through a filter of racial experience. That can cause problems," he says. "But, you know," he adds with a shrug, "I've been straddling this line most of my life."

But is it possible to get past all that? "I don't believe it is possible to transcend race in this country," Obama responds, ready for the question. "Race is a factor in this society. The legacy of Jim Crow and slavery has not gone away. It is not an accident that African-Americans experience high crime rates, are poor, and have less wealth. It is a direct result of our racial history."

Ambitious and driven as any presidential candidate must be, Obama is definitely playing with the big boys now. Thanks to an earlier publicity boom—shirtless and caught unaware in *People* magazine, well-suited and very aware in *Men's Vogue*—he has millions of dollars in political contributions in the bank. Moreover, a *Newsweek* poll earlier this year found that 59 percent of Americans feel we are ready for a Black president, up from 37 percent in 2000. But what Americans tell poll takers, and what they do in the voting booth next year, remains an open question.

Cassandra Butts, a law school classmate of Obama's who is now an informal adviser, says the senator from Illinois is uniquely positioned to turn what some see as his negatives—race, youth, inexperience—into positives.

"He has had to be in both places," she says, referring to his biracial background. "He's had to figure out how to synthesize and come to terms with two competing realities."

Maybe so, but I've covered a lot of campaigns, and I've never fielded so many questions about a candidate from so many different people. White voters ask me, Is America ready to elect him? Black voters ask me, Are African-Americans ready? I asked Barack's wife, Michelle, what I should tell Black folks, especially older ones, who say that they fear for her husband's safety. "You tell 'em like I tell my mother, to not make a choice based on fear," she replied. "If you focus on the fear, you do nothing. You're frozen in place. And we've been frozen in place for too long."

Obama's boosters certainly appear fearless. Cornell Belcher, the African-American pollster conducting surveys for Obama, insists it is all a matter of introducing the candidate properly. "The truth is, four years ago the average African-American didn't know who Barack Obama was," he tells me. "So we're filling in that profile."

The bare bones of that profile is a by-his-bootstraps story with apparently broad resonance. The absent father. The single mother. First Black president of the *Harvard Law Review*. Then, in quick succession, a career as a lawyer, then community organizer, then state senator, and finally, as only the fifth Black elected U.S. senator.

But the most dramatic chapter may still be unwritten. "As president, obviously the day I am inaugurated, the racial dynamics in this country will change to some degree. If you've got Michelle as first lady, and Malia and Sasha running around on the South Lawn, that changes how America looks at itself. It changes how White children think about Black children, and it changes how Black children think about Black children," he says.

I spent a fair amount of 1988 following another Black presidential candidate around the country. The Reverend Jesse Jackson was making his second bid for the White House, taking a hammer to the glass ceiling of presidential politics. Jackson now says he supports Obama, but the two men and their campaigns could not be more different. Obama is a loyal and committed member of the Trinity United Church of Christ in Chicago, but he is not the charismatic preacher that Jackson is. His speeches are more academic than rhythmic, more studied than street. Where Jackson raised campaign cash passing collection plates in Black churches, Obama's fund-raisers are more likely to take place in the leafy backyard of a well-heeled New Hampshire supporter or at Oprah

Winfrey's sumptuous Santa Barbara estate. Obama's idea of a quick lunch is bottled water, trail mix and bananas. With Jackson, it was soul food all day, every day. Near the end of the 1988 campaign, the press corps sprung for T-shirts printed with the image of a chicken—with a red slash through it. I swore off fried poultry for a year.

And because race is never far from the center of the conversation for any Black candidate, another consequential difference is worth noting. Unless Obama is speaking before the NAACP, at a Tavis Smiley–led debate at Howard University, or at the National Urban League or the NABJ—as he did in rapid succession this summer—most of his crowds are White. And although his pollster, policy director and political director are all African-American men, most of his campaign staff is White, too. Therein lies a challenge for the man a *Washington Monthly* cover story crowned "The Great Black Hope" the minute he arrived in Washington in 2004.

I ask the candidate directly, "Does Barack Obama really believe America is ready for a Black president?"

"I think that racial attitudes have changed sufficiently in this country, that people are willing to vote for me for president," he responds, "if they think I can help them on health care, on education, on the issues that are important in their lives." Still, he isn't wearing blinders. "Now, are there going to be people who don't vote for me because I am Black? Absolutely," he continues. "But I do not believe those are people who would have voted for me, given my political philosophy, even if I were White."

To win, Obama is going to have to defy a lot of history. Shirley Chisholm, the outspoken, bespectacled congresswoman from Brooklyn, won 152 delegates when she ran for president. Al Sharpton, Alan Keyes and Carol Moseley Braun also made quixotic swipes at the crown, only to fade by autumn. Jackson won 3.5 million votes in his first run in 1984 and delivered a memorable prime-time speech at that year's Democratic National Convention. By 1988 he had nearly doubled that tally, collecting enough delegates to keep hope alive right up until the party nominated Michael Dukakis in Atlanta.

Jackson, in a candid interview, suggests he has endorsed Obama this time around only because they are both from Illinois. It turns out he remembers an episode in 1988 when the late Paul Simon dropped out of the primary campaign but refused to release his delegates to fellow Illinois resident Jackson. By supporting Obama, Jackson says he is granting the favor he was denied 20 years ago.

Jackson attributes Obama's success to the groundwork his 1980's campaigns laid from the bottom up with grassroots organizing. Obama's effort today, he says pointedly, is "top down," reaping the benefit of an establishment embrace bestowed after his 2004 convention speech. "I think the campaign is trying to distinguish itself as different from our campaign," he says. Asked if he will campaign for Obama, he grows cautious. "I don't know about that," he says. "I have not been asked to campaign."

Obama rejects comparisons to Jackson or to Sharpton, who so far has declined to support the senator. But don't expect Obama to criticize either of them. "That's an old game to pit one group of Blacks against the other," he says. In fact, he says he consulted Jackson before he decided to run. " 'Barack, we had to break the door down,' " Obama recalls Jackson saying. " 'Which means sometimes you're not polite. You get bloodied up a little bit. You haven't had to go through that, and that's a good thing.' "

Still, Obama has his battles to fight.

Is this Black man with a Black wife and Black daughters "Black enough"? The question has never quite seemed to go away since he hit the national scene. Obama—without being asked—wondered aloud at the journalists' conference why it is so persistent when it never came up earlier in his career.

Is he still dealing with that question? "I'm done with it," Obama says laughing. "I don't know 'bout y'all; I'm sure not confused about it. And the truth is, I don't think most folks are. Most of the folks in my barbershop are not confused about it."

But other questions loom, many fanned by competing campaigns, such as, Does he have enough experience? Belcher says Obama brings a different kind of experience to the table. "This is a guy who left Harvard and went back to the 'hood to organize," he says. "Has he been in Washington for 20 years? No," he says. "And I think voters are tired of that kind of experience."

But, can he speak truth to power as he has to the powerless? Although clearly an antiwar liberal, Obama has used debates and speeches to challenge the accepted orthodoxy of his own race and party. While scolding African-Americans for homophobia and Black-on-Black crime, he angered peace activists by suggesting he would use force, if necessary, to pursue terrorists.

Dyson thinks Obama has room to attract even as he alienates, especially on racial ground. No one, he points out, can talk about family, like family. "But when you do that kind of thing, you have a corollary responsibility to take on issues that White candidates might not speak to, that it is now incumbent upon you to do."

Michelle Obama, who met her husband in the summer of 1988 when both worked for a Chicago law firm, remains his closest adviser. She warns against expecting too much from the so-called Great Black Hope who draws comparisons to the Kennedys. "You cannot wait for Barack to emote us into change," she told me earlier this year. "He's going to stumble. He's gonna make mistakes."

Stumbles and mistakes have surfaced, including his financial ties to a controversial Chicago businessman, and forced apologies for campaign missteps. But Obama has also stepped up his game in recent months, with sharper speeches and more pointed attacks. In one famous late-summer dustup, Senator Clinton called him "naive and irresponsible" for suggesting that, as president, he would meet with leaders of rogue nations. He responded with a fierce comeback, charging that she was the naive one for originally voting to support the war in Iraq he opposed. Yet Obama has had some trouble carving out clear ground for himself. John Edwards has worked to outflank him in the South and on traditional issues like poverty. Clinton has outshone him elsewhere, lining up Black support from the likes of Magic Johnson and Quincy Jones. More than one Black official on the fence received friendly nudging calls from her popular husband, Bill. "I don't begrudge them that," Obama says. "Because the relationships are what they are."

On domestic issues, especially those dear to Black Americans, there is less clear difference. Like most Democrats, he favors raising the minimum wage and boosting funds for HIV/AIDS prevention.

But Obama must now convince voters he stands apart from his rivals.

"I'm not afraid to lose," he tells me. "When Michelle and I talked about this, our attitude was, it's only worth it if we get out of this whole on the other end; if we haven't given up who we are; if we're pushing the envelope a little."

I've never been quite able to believe a candidate who says he doesn't mind losing. As his own daughter might say, the pressure involved in a presidential campaign is way too great. But then again, I've never seen Obama sweat.

This article first appeared in the October 2007 issue of ESSENCE.

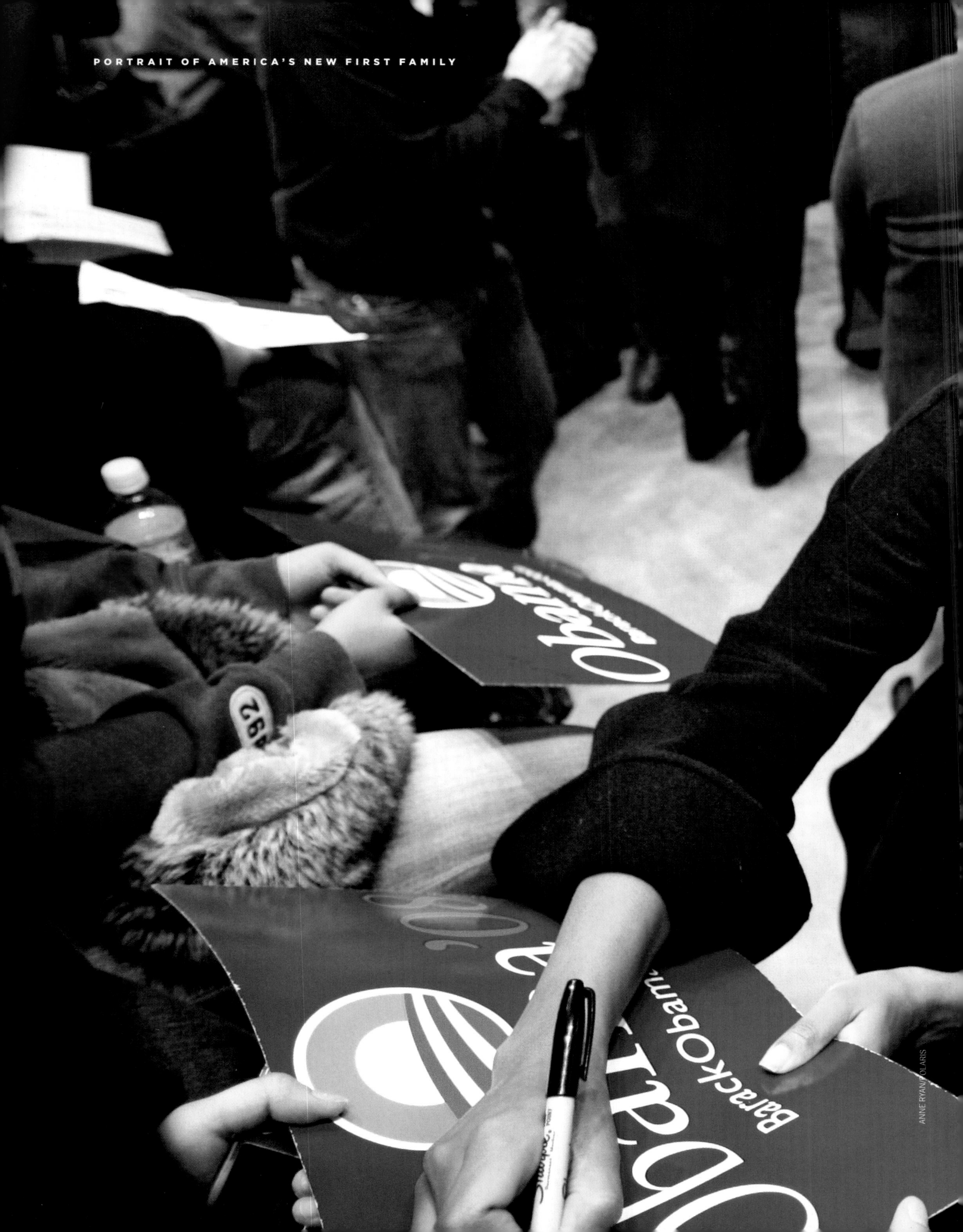

ANNE RYAN/POLARIS

BarackObama.com

Obama '08

Michelle signs
Obama campaign
posters at a rally in
Ames, Iowa. Barack
had announced his
candidacy earlier that
day, February 11, 2007.

"A MORE PERFECT UNION"

On March 18, 2008, Senator Barack Obama delivered a pivotal oration on race at the National Constitution Center in Philadelphia in the wake of previous controversial remarks made by his former pastor Rev. Jeremiah Wright of Chicago's Trinity United Church of Christ

We the people, in order to form a more perfect union."

Two hundred and twenty-one years ago, in a hall that still stands across the street, a group of men gathered and, with these simple words, launched America's improbable experiment in democracy. Farmers and scholars; statesmen and patriots who had traveled across an ocean to escape tyranny and persecution finally made real their declaration of independence at a Philadelphia convention that lasted through the spring of 1787.

The document they produced was eventually signed but ultimately unfinished. It was stained by this nation's original sin of slavery, a question that divided the colonies and brought the convention to a stalemate until the founders chose to allow the slave trade to continue for at least 20 more years, and to leave any final resolution to future generations.

Of course, the answer to the slavery question was already embedded within our Constitution - a Constitution that had at its very core the ideal of equal citizenship under the law; a Constitution that promised its people liberty, and justice, and a union that could be and should be perfected over time.

And yet words on a parchment would not be enough to deliver slaves from bondage, or provide men and women of every color and creed their full rights and obligations as citizens of the United States. What would be needed were Americans in successive generations who were willing to do their part - through protests and struggle, on the streets and in the courts, through a civil war and civil disobedience and always at great risk - to narrow that gap between the promise of our ideals and the reality of their time.

This was one of the tasks we set forth at the beginning of this campaign - to continue the long march of those who came before us, a march for a more just, more equal, more free, more caring and more prosperous America. I chose to run for the presidency at this moment in history because I believe deeply that we cannot solve the challenges of our time unless we solve them together - unless we perfect our union by understanding that we may have different stories, but we hold common hopes; that we may not look the same and we may not have come from the same place, but we all want to move in the same direction - toward a better future for our children and our grandchildren.

This belief comes from my unyielding faith in the decency and generosity of the American people. But it also comes from my own American story.

I am the son of a black man from Kenya and a white woman from Kansas. I was raised with the help of a white grandfather who survived a depression to serve in Patton's Army during World War II and a white grandmother who worked on a bomber assembly line at Fort Leavenworth while he was overseas. I've gone to some of the best schools in America and lived in one of the world's poorest nations. I am married to a black American who carries within her the blood of slaves and slave owners - an inheritance we pass on to our two precious daughters. I have brothers, sisters, nieces, nephews, uncles and cousins, of every race and every hue, scattered across three continents, and for as long as I live, I will never forget that in no other country on earth is my story even possible.

It's a story that hasn't made me the most conventional candidate. But it is a story that has seared into my genetic makeup the idea that this nation is more than the sum of its parts - that out of many, we are truly one.

Throughout the first year of this campaign, against all predictions to the contrary, we saw how hungry the American people were for this message of unity. Despite the temptation to view my candidacy through a purely racial lens, we won commanding victories in states with some of the whitest populations in the country. In South Carolina, where the Confederate flag still flies, we built a powerful coalition of African-Americans and white Americans.

This is not to say that race has not been an issue in the campaign. At various stages in the campaign, some commentators have deemed me either "too black" or "not black enough." We saw racial tensions bubble to the surface during the week before the South Carolina primary. The press has scoured every exit poll for the latest evidence of racial polarization, not just in terms of white and black, but black and brown as well.

And yet, it has only been in the last couple of weeks that the discussion of race in this campaign has taken a particularly divisive turn.

On one end of the spectrum, we've heard the implication that my candidacy is somehow an exercise in affirmative action; that it's based solely on the desire of wide-eyed liberals to purchase racial reconciliation on the cheap. On the other end, we've heard my former pastor, Rev. Jeremiah Wright, use incendiary language to express views that have the potential not only to widen the racial divide, but views that denigrate both the greatness and the goodness of our nation; that rightly offend white and black alike.

I have already condemned, in unequivocal terms, the statements of Reverend Wright that have caused such controversy. For some, nagging questions remain. Did I know him to be an occasionally fierce critic of American domestic and foreign policy? Of course. Did I ever hear him make remarks that could be considered controversial while I sat in church? Yes. Did I strongly disagree with many of his political views? Absolutely - just as I'm sure many of you have heard remarks from your pastors, priests, or rabbis with which you strongly disagreed.

But the remarks that have caused this recent firestorm weren't simply controversial. They weren't simply a religious leader's effort to speak out against perceived injustice. Instead, they expressed a profoundly distorted view of this country - a view that sees white racism as endemic, and that elevates what is wrong with America above all that we know is right with America; a view that sees the conflicts in the Middle East as rooted primarily in the actions of stalwart allies like Israel, instead of emanating from the perverse and hateful ideologies of radical Islam.

As such, Reverend Wright's comments were not only wrong but divisive, divisive at a time when we need unity; racially charged at a time when we need to come together to solve a set of monumental problems - two wars, a terrorist threat, a falling economy, a chronic health care crisis and potentially devastating climate change; problems that are neither black or white or Latino or Asian, but rather problems that confront us all.

Given my background, my politics, and my professed values and ideals, there will no doubt be those for whom my statements of condemnation are not enough. Why associate myself with Reverend Wright in the first place, they may ask? Why not join another church? And I confess that if all that I knew of Reverend Wright were the snippets of those sermons that have run in an endless loop on the television and YouTube, or if Trinity United Church of Christ conformed to the caricatures being peddled by some commentators, there is no doubt that I would react in much the same way.

But the truth is, that isn't all that I know of the man. The man I met more than 20 years ago is a man who helped introduce me to my Christian faith, a man who spoke to me about our obligations to love one another; to care for the sick and lift up the poor. He is a man who served his country as a U.S. Marine; who has studied and lectured at some of the finest universities and seminaries in the country, and who for over 30 years led a church that serves the community by doing God's work here on earth - by housing the homeless, ministering to the needy, providing day care services and scholarships and prison ministries, and reaching out to those suffering from HIV/AIDS.

In my first book, *Dreams From My Father*, I described the experience of my first service at Trinity: "People began to shout, to rise from their seats and clap and cry out, a forceful wind carrying the reverend's voice up into the rafters.... And in that single note - hope! - I heard something else; at the foot of that cross, inside the thousands of churches across the city, I imagined the stories of ordinary black people merging with the stories of David and Goliath, Moses and Pharaoh, the Christians in the lion's den, Ezekiel's field of dry bones. Those stories - of survival, and freedom, and hope - became our story, my story; the blood that had spilled was our blood, the tears our tears; until this black church, on this bright day, seemed once more a vessel carrying the story of a people into future generations and into a larger world. Our trials and triumphs became at once unique and universal, black and more than black; in chronicling our journey, the stories and songs gave us a means to reclaim memories that we didn't need to feel shame about...memories that all people might study and cherish - and with which we could start to rebuild."

That has been my experience at Trinity. Like other predominantly black churches across the country, Trinity embodies the black community in its entirety - the doctor and the welfare mom, the model student and the former gangbanger. Like other black churches, Trinity's services are full of raucous laughter and sometimes bawdy humor. They are full of dancing, clapping, screaming and shouting that may seem jarring to the untrained ear. The church contains in full the kindness and cruelty, the fierce intelligence and the shocking ignorance, the struggles and successes, the love and yes, the bitterness and bias that make up the black experience in America.

And this helps explain, perhaps, my relationship with Reverend Wright. As imperfect as he may be, he has been like family to me. He strengthened my faith, officiated my wedding, and baptized my children. Not once in my conversations with him have I heard him talk about any ethnic group in derogatory terms, or treat whites with whom he interacted with anything but courtesy and respect. He contains within him the contradictions - the good and the bad - of the community that he has served diligently for so many years.

I can no more disown him than I can disown the black community. I can no more disown him than I can my white grandmother - a woman who helped raise me, a woman who sacrificed again and again for me, a woman who loves me as much as she loves anything in this world, but a woman who once confessed her fear of black men who passed by her on the street, and who on more than one occasion has uttered racial or ethnic stereotypes that made me cringe.

These people are a part of me. And they are a part of America, this country that I love.

Some will see this as an attempt to justify or excuse comments that are simply inexcusable. I can assure you it is not. I suppose the politically safe thing would be to move on from this episode and just hope that it fades into the woodwork. We can dismiss Reverend Wright as a crank or a demagogue, just as some have dismissed Geraldine Ferraro, in the aftermath of her recent statements, as harboring some deep-seated racial bias.

But race is an issue that I believe this nation cannot afford to ignore right now. We would be making the same mistake that Reverend Wright made in his offending sermons about America - to simplify and stereotype and amplify the negative to the point that it distorts reality.

The fact is that the comments that have been made and the issues that have surfaced over the last few weeks reflect the complexities of race in this country that we've never really worked through - a part of our union that we have yet to perfect. And if we walk away now, if we simply retreat into our respective corners, we will never be able to come together and solve challenges like health care, or education, or the need to find good jobs for every American.

Understanding this reality requires a reminder of how we arrived at this point. As William Faulkner once wrote, "The past isn't dead and buried. In fact, it isn't even past." We do not need to recite here the history of racial injustice in this country. But we do need to remind ourselves that so many of the disparities that exist in the African-American community today can be directly traced to inequalities passed on from an earlier generation that suffered under the brutal legacy of slavery and Jim Crow.

Segregated schools were, and are, inferior schools; we still haven't fixed them, 50 years after *Brown* v. *Board of Education*, and the inferior education they provided, then and now, helps explain the pervasive achievement gap between today's black and white students.

Legalized discrimination - where blacks were prevented, often through violence, from owning property, or loans were not granted to African-American business owners, or black home owners could not access FHA mortgages, or blacks were excluded from unions, or the police force, or fire departments - meant that black families could not amass any meaningful wealth to bequeath to future generations. That history helps explain the wealth and income gap between black and white, and the concentrated pockets of poverty that persists in so many of today's urban and rural communities.

A lack of economic opportunity among black men, and the shame and frustration that came from not being able to provide for one's family, contributed to the erosion of black families - a problem that welfare policies for many years may have worsened. And the lack of basic services in so many urban black neighborhoods - parks for kids to play in, police walking the beat, regular garbage pickup and building code enforcement - all helped create a cycle of violence, blight and neglect that continue to haunt us. This is the reality in which Reverend Wright and other African-Americans of his generation grew up. They came of age in the late fifties and early sixties, a time when segregation was still the law of the land and opportunity was systematically constricted.

What's remarkable is not how many failed in the face of discrimination, but rather how many men and women overcame the odds; how many were able to make a way out of no way for those like me who would come after them.

But for all those who scratched and clawed their way to get a piece of the American Dream, there were many who didn't make it - those who were ultimately defeated, in one way or another, by discrimination. That legacy of defeat was passed on to future generations - those young men and increasingly young women who we see standing on street corners or languishing in our prisons, without hope or prospects for the future. Even for those blacks who did make it, questions of race, and racism, continue to define their worldview in fundamental ways. For the men and women of Reverend Wright's generation, the memories of humiliation and doubt and fear have not gone away; nor has the anger and the bitterness of those years. That anger may not get expressed in public, in front of white coworkers or white friends. But it does find voice in the barbershop or around the kitchen table. At times, that anger is exploited by politicians, to gin up votes along racial lines, or to make up for a politician's own failings.

And occasionally it finds voice in the church on Sunday morning, in the pulpit and in the pews. The fact that so many people are surprised to hear that anger in some of Reverend Wright's sermons simply reminds us of the old truism that the most segregated hour in American life occurs on Sunday morning. That anger is not always productive; indeed, all too often it distracts attention from solving real problems; it keeps us from squarely facing our own complicity in our condition, and prevents the African-American community from forging the alliances it needs to bring about real change. But the anger is real; it is powerful; and to simply wish it away, to condemn it without understanding its roots, only serves to widen the chasm of misunderstanding that exists between the races.

In fact, a similar anger exists within segments of the white community. Most working- and middle-class white Americans don't feel that they have been particularly privileged by their race. Their experience is the immigrant experience - as far as they're concerned, no one's handed them anything, they've built it from scratch. They've worked hard all their lives, many times only to see their jobs shipped overseas or their pension dumped after a lifetime of labor. They are anxious about their futures, and feel their dreams slipping away; in an era of stagnant wages and global competition, opportunity comes to be seen as a zero-sum game, in which your dreams come at my expense. So when they are told to bus their children to a school across town; when they hear that an African-American is getting an advantage in landing a good job or a spot in a good college because of an injustice that they themselves never committed; when they're told that their fears about crime in urban neighborhoods are somehow prejudiced, resentment builds over time.

Like the anger within the black community, these resentments aren't always expressed in polite company. But they have helped shape the political landscape for at least a generation. Anger over welfare and affirmative action helped forge the Reagan coalition. Politicians routinely exploited fears of crime for their own electoral ends. Talk show hosts and conservative commentators built entire careers unmasking bogus claims of racism while dismissing legitimate discussions of racial injustice and inequality as mere political correctness or reverse racism.

Just as black anger often proved counterproductive, so have these white resentments distracted attention from the real culprits of the middle-class squeeze - a corporate culture rife with inside dealing, questionable accounting practices, and short-term greed; a Washington dominated by lobbyists and special interests; economic policies that favor the few over the many. And yet, to wish away the resentments of white Americans, to label them as misguided or even racist, without recognizing they are grounded in legitimate concerns - this too widens the racial divide, and blocks the path to understanding.

This is where we are right now. It's a racial stalemate we've been stuck in for years. Contrary to the claims of some of my critics, black and white, I have never been so naive as to believe that we can get beyond our racial divisions in a single election cycle, or with a single candidacy - particularly a candidacy as imperfect as my own.

But I have asserted a firm conviction - a conviction rooted in my faith in God and my faith in the American people - that working together we can move beyond some of our old racial wounds, and

U.S. Democratic presidential candidate Senator Barack Obama (D-IL) spoke about the role race has played in his life, the presidential campaign and America during a crucial event at the National Constitution Center in Philadelphia. Obama challenged Rev. Jeremiah Wright, his former pastor, for racially charged rhetoric that had come to light. But the candidate also said he could not disown him, March 18, 2008.

that in fact we have no choice if we are to continue on the path of a more perfect union.

For the African-American community, that path means embracing the burdens of our past without becoming victims of our past. It means continuing to insist on a full measure of justice in every aspect of American life. But it also means binding our particular grievances - for better health care, and better schools, and better jobs - to the larger aspirations of all Americans - the white woman struggling to break the glass ceiling, the white man who has been laid off, the immigrant trying to feed his family. And it means taking full responsibility for our own lives - by demanding more from our fathers, and spending more time with our children, and reading to them, and teaching them that while they may face challenges and discrimination in their own lives, they must never succumb to despair or cynicism; they must always believe that they can write their own destiny.

Ironically, this quintessentially American - and yes, conservative - notion of self-help found frequent expression in Reverend Wright's sermons. But what my former pastor too often failed to understand is that embarking on a program of self-help also requires a belief that society can change.

The profound mistake of Reverend Wright's sermons is not that he spoke about racism in our society. It's that he spoke as if our society was static; as if no progress has been made; as if this country - a country that has made it possible for one of his own members to run for the highest office in the land and build a coalition of white and black; Latino and Asian, rich and poor, young and old - is still irrevocably bound to a tragic past. But what we know - what we have seen - is that America can change. That is the true genius of this nation. What we have already achieved gives us hope - the audacity to hope - for what we can and must achieve tomorrow.

In the white community, the path to a more perfect union means acknowledging that what ails the African-American community does not just exist in the minds of black people; that the legacy of discrimination - and current incidents of discrimination, while less overt than in the past - are real and must be addressed. Not just with words, but with deeds - by investing in our schools and our communities; by enforcing our civil rights laws and ensuring fairness in our criminal justice system; by providing this generation with ladders of opportunity that were unavailable for previous generations.

Michelle Obama, along with (from far left) Eric Holder, Valerie Jarrett and Marty Nesbitt, listens as Obama delivers his history-making speech on race at the National Constitution Center in Philadelphia, March 18, 2008.

SCOUT TUFANKJIAN / POLARIS

It requires all Americans to realize that your dreams do not have to come at the expense of my dreams; that investing in the health, welfare, and education of black and brown and white children will ultimately help all of America prosper.

In the end, then, what is called for is nothing more, and nothing less, than what all the world's great religions demand - that we do unto others as we would have them do unto us. Let us be our brother's keeper, Scripture tells us. Let us be our sister's keeper. Let us find that common stake we all have in one another, and let our politics reflect that spirit as well.

For we have a choice in this country. We can accept a politics that breeds division, and conflict, and cynicism. We can tackle race only as spectacle - as we did in the O.J. trial - or in the wake of tragedy, as we did in the aftermath of Katrina - or as fodder for the nightly news.

We can play Reverend Wright's sermons on every channel, every day and talk about them from now until the election, and make the only question in this campaign whether or not the American people think that I somehow believe or sympathize with his most offensive words.

We can pounce on some gaffe by a Hillary supporter as evidence that she's playing the race card, or we can speculate on whether white men will all flock to John McCain in the general election regardless of his policies.

We can do that.

But if we do, I can tell you that in the next election, we'll be talking about some other distraction. And then another one. And then another one. And nothing will change.

That is one option. Or, at this moment, in this election, we can come together and say, "Not this time." This time we want to talk about the crumbling schools that are stealing the future of black children and white children and Asian children and Hispanic children and Native American children. This time we want to reject the cynicism that tells us that these kids can't learn; that those kids who don't look like us are somebody else's problem. The children of America are not those kids, they are our kids, and we will not let them fall behind in a twenty-first-century economy. Not this time.

This time we want to talk about how the lines in the emergency room are filled with whites and blacks and Hispanics who do not have health care; who don't have the power on their own to overcome the special interests in Washington, but who can take them on if we do it together.

This time we want to talk about the shuttered mills that once provided a decent life for men and women of every race, and the homes for sale that once belonged to Americans from every religion, every region, every walk of life. This time we want to talk about the fact that the real problem is not that someone who doesn't look like you might take your job; it's that the corporation you work for will ship it overseas for nothing more than a profit.

This time we want to talk about the men and women of every color and creed who serve together, and fight together, and bleed together under the same proud flag. We want to talk about how to bring them home from a war that never should've been authorized and never should've been waged, and we want to talk about how we'll show our patriotism by caring for them, and their families, and giving them the benefits they have earned.

I would not be running for president if I didn't believe with all my heart that this is what the vast majority of Americans want for this country. This union may never be perfect, but generation after generation has shown that it can always be perfected. And today, whenever I find myself feeling doubtful or cynical about this possibility, what gives me the most hope is the next generation - the young people whose attitudes and beliefs and openness to change have already made history in this election.

There is one story in particular that I'd like to leave you with today - a story I told when I had the great honor of speaking on Dr. King's birthday at his home church, Ebenezer Baptist, in Atlanta.

There is a young, 23-year-old white woman named Ashley Baia who organized for our campaign in Florence, South Carolina.

She had been working to organize a mostly African-American community since the beginning of this campaign, and one day she was at a roundtable discussion where everyone went around telling their story and why they were there.

And Ashley said that when she was 9 years old, her mother got cancer. And because she had to miss days of work, she was let go and lost her health care.

They had to file for bankruptcy, and that's when Ashley decided that she had to do something to help her mom.

She knew that food was one of their most expensive costs, and so Ashley convinced her mother that what she really liked and really wanted to eat more than anything else was mustard and relish sandwiches. Because that was the cheapest way to eat.

She did this for a year until her mom got better, and she told everyone at the roundtable that the reason she joined our campaign was so that she could help the millions of other children in the country who want and need to help their parents too.

Now Ashley might have made a different choice. Perhaps somebody told her along the way that the source of her mother's problems were blacks who were on welfare and too lazy to work, or Hispanics who were coming into the country illegally. But she didn't. She sought out allies in her fight against injustice.

Anyway, Ashley finishes her story and then goes around the room and asks everyone else why they're supporting the campaign.

They all have different stories and reasons.

Many bring up a specific issue. And finally they come to this elderly black man who's been sitting there quietly the entire time. And Ashley asks him why he's there.

And he does not bring up a specific issue. He does not say health care or the economy. He does not say education or the war. He does not say that he was there because of Barack Obama.

He simply says to everyone in the room, "I am here because of Ashley."

"I'm here because of Ashley."

By itself, that single moment of recognition between that young white girl and that old black man is not enough. It is not enough to give health care to the sick, or jobs to the jobless, or education to our children.

But it is where we start. It is where our union grows stronger.

And as so many generations have come to realize over the course of the 221 years since a band of patriots signed that document in Philadelphia, that is where the perfection begins.

Teasing a staffer whose job
is to keep the press back,
Obama marches with supporters
to an event in Indianola, Iowa,
where he and other Democratic
presidential contenders
spoke on a range of issues,
September 16, 2007.

Michelle and Barack just before his pivotal speech in St. Paul after he clinched the Democratic nomination, June 3, 2008.

Robert Carey, 7, is at the Obama campaign office in Memphis, where he helps his mother the day early voting began in Tennessee, October 14, 2008.

—— • SPEECH • ——

"THE AMERICAN PROMISE"

On August 28, 2008, Senator Barack Obama became the first African-American to head a major political party's presidential ticket. He accepted the nomination to thunderous applause during the close of the Democratic National Convention in Denver

To Chairman Dean and my great friend Dick Durbin; and to all my fellow citizens of this great nation;

With profound gratitude and great humility, I accept your nomination for the presidency of the United States.

Let me express my thanks to the historic slate of candidates who accompanied me on this journey, and especially the one who traveled the farthest - a champion for working Americans and an inspiration to my daughters and to yours - Hillary Rodham Clinton. To President Clinton, who last night made the case for change as only he can make it; to Ted Kennedy, who embodies the spirit of service; and to the next Vice President of the United States, Joe Biden, I thank you. I am grateful to finish this journey with one of the finest statesmen of our time, a man at ease with everyone from world leaders to the conductors on the Amtrak train he still takes home every night.

To the love of my life, our next First Lady, Michelle Obama, and to Sasha and Malia - I love you so much, and I'm so proud of all of you.

Four years ago, I stood before you and told you my story - of the brief union between a young man from Kenya and a young woman from Kansas who weren't well-off or well-known, but shared a belief that in America, their son could achieve whatever he put his mind to.

It is that promise that has always set this country apart - that through hard work and sacrifice, each of us can pursue our individual dreams but still come together as one American family, to ensure that the next generation can pursue their dreams as well.

That's why I stand here tonight. Because for 232 years, at each moment when that promise was in jeopardy, ordinary men and women - students and soldiers, farmers and teachers, nurses and janitors - found the courage to keep it alive.

We meet at one of those defining moments - a moment when our nation is at war, our economy is in turmoil, and the American promise has been threatened once more.

Tonight, more Americans are out of work and more are working harder for less. More of you have lost your homes and even more are watching your home values plummet. More of you have cars you can't afford to drive, credit card bills you can't afford to pay, and tuition that's beyond your reach.

These challenges are not all of government's making. But the failure to respond is a direct result of a broken politics in Washington and the failed policies of George W. Bush.

America, we are better than these last eight years. We are a better country than this.

This country is more decent than one where a woman in Ohio, on the brink of retirement, finds herself one illness away from disaster after a lifetime of hard work.

This country is more generous than one where a man in Indiana has to pack up the equipment he's worked on for 20 years and watch it shipped off to China, and then chokes up as he explains how he felt like a failure when he went home to tell his family the news.

We are more compassionate than a government that lets veterans sleep on our streets and families slide into poverty; that sits on its hands while a major American city drowns before our eyes.

Tonight, I say to the American people, to Democrats and Republicans and Independents across this great land - enough! This moment - this election - is our chance to keep, in the twenty-first century, the American promise alive. Because next week, in Minnesota, the same party that brought you two terms of George Bush and Dick Cheney will ask this country for a third. And we are here because we love this country too much to let the next four years look like the last eight. On November 4, we must stand up and say: "Eight is enough."

Now let there be no doubt. The Republican nominee, John McCain, has worn the uniform of our country with bravery and distinction, and for that we owe him our gratitude and respect. And next week, we'll also hear about those occasions when he's broken with his party as evidence that he can deliver the change that we need.

But the record's clear: John McCain has voted with George Bush 90 percent of the time. Senator McCain likes to talk about judgment, but really, what does it say about your judgment when you think George Bush has been right more than 90 percent of the time? I don't know about you, but I'm not ready to take a 10 percent chance on change.

The truth is, on issue after issue that would make a difference in your lives - on health care and education and the economy - Senator McCain has been anything but independent. He said that our economy has made "great progress" under this President. He said that the fundamentals of the economy are strong. And when one of his chief advisers - the man who wrote his economic plan - was talking about the anxiety Americans are feeling, he said that we were just suffering from a "mental recession," and that we've become, and I quote, "a nation of whiners." A nation of whiners? Tell that to the proud auto workers at a Michigan plant who, after they found out it was closing, kept showing up every day and working as hard as ever, because they knew there were people who counted on the brakes that they made. Tell that to the military families who shoulder their burdens silently as they watch their loved ones leave for their third or fourth or fifth tour of duty. These are not whiners. They work hard and give back and keep going without complaint. These are the Americans that I know.

Now, I don't believe that Senator McCain doesn't care what's going on in the lives of Americans. I just think he doesn't know. Why else would he define middle class as someone making under $5 million a year? How else could he propose hundreds of billions in tax breaks for big corporations and oil companies but not one penny of tax relief to more than 100 million Americans? How else could he offer a health care plan that would actually tax people's benefits, or an education plan that would do nothing to help families pay for college, or a plan that would privatize Social Security and gamble your retirement?

It's not because John McCain doesn't care. It's because John McCain doesn't get it.

For over two decades, he's subscribed to that old, discredited Republican philosophy - give more and more to those with the most and hope that prosperity trickles down to everyone else. In Washington, they call this the Ownership Society, but what it really means is - you're on your own. Out of work? Tough luck. No health care? The market will fix it. Born into poverty? Pull yourself up by your own bootstraps - even if you don't have boots. You're on your own.

Well it's time for them to own their failure. It's time for us to change America.

You see, we Democrats have a very different measure of what constitutes progress in this country.

We measure progress by how many people can find a job that pays the mortgage; whether you can put a little extra money away at the end of each month so you can someday watch your child receive her college diploma. We measure progress in the 23 million new jobs that were created when Bill Clinton was president - when the average American family saw its income go up $7,500 instead of down $2,000 like it has under George Bush.

We measure the strength of our economy not by the number of billionaires we have or the profits of the Fortune 500, but by whether someone with a good idea can take a risk and start a new business, or whether the waitress who lives on tips can take a day off to look after a sick kid without losing her job - an economy that honors the dignity of work.

The fundamentals we use to measure economic strength are whether we are living up to that fundamental promise that has made this country great - a promise that is the only reason I am standing here tonight.

Because in the faces of those young veterans who come back from Iraq and Afghanistan, I see my grandfather, who signed up after Pearl Harbor, marched in Patton's Army, and was rewarded by a grateful nation with the chance to go to college on the GI Bill.

In the face of that young student who sleeps just three hours before working the night shift, I think about my mom, who raised my sister and me on her own while she worked and earned her degree; who once turned to food stamps but was still able to send us to the best schools in the country with the help of student loans and scholarships.

When I listen to another worker tell me that his factory has shut down, I remember all those men and women on the South Side of Chicago who I stood by and fought for two decades ago after the local steel plant closed.

And when I hear a woman talk about the difficulties of starting her own business, I think about my grandmother, who worked her way up from the secretarial pool to middle management, despite years of being passed over for promotions because she was a woman. She's the one who taught me about hard work. She's the one who put off buying a new car or a new dress for herself so that I could have a better life. She poured everything she had into me. And although she can no longer travel, I know that she's watching tonight, and that tonight is her night as well.

I don't know what kind of lives John McCain thinks that celebrities lead, but this has been mine. These are my heroes. Theirs are the stories that shaped me. And it is on their behalf that I intend to win this election and keep our promise alive as president of the United States. What is that promise?

It's a promise that says each of us has the freedom to make of our own lives what we will, but that we also have the obligation to treat each other with dignity and respect.

It's a promise that says the market should reward drive and innovation and generate growth, but that businesses should live up to their responsibilities to create American jobs, look out for American workers, and play by the rules of the road.

Ours is a promise that says government cannot solve all our problems, but what it should do is that which we cannot do for ourselves - protect us from harm and provide every child a decent education; keep our water clean and our toys safe; invest in new schools and new roads and new science and technology.

Our government should work for us, not against us. It should help us, not hurt us. It should ensure opportunity not just for those with the most money and influence, but for every American who's willing to work.

That's the promise of America - the idea that we are responsible for ourselves, but that we also rise or fall as one nation; the fundamental belief that I am my brother's keeper; I am my sister's keeper.

That's the promise we need to keep. That's the change we need right now. So let me spell out exactly what that change would mean if I am president.

Change means a tax code that doesn't reward the lobbyists who wrote it, but the American workers and small businesses who deserve it.

Unlike John McCain, I will stop giving tax breaks to corporations that ship jobs overseas, and I will start giving them to companies that create good jobs right here in America.

I will eliminate capital gains taxes for the small businesses and the start-ups that will create the high-wage, high-tech jobs of tomorrow.

I will cut taxes - cut taxes - for 95 percent of all working families. Because in an economy like this, the last thing we should do is raise taxes on the middle class.

And for the sake of our economy, our security, and the future of our planet, I will set a clear goal as president: In ten years, we will finally end our dependence on oil from the Middle East.

Washington's been talking about our oil addiction for the last 30 years, and John McCain has been there for 26 of them. In that time, he's said no to higher fuel-efficiency standards for cars, no to investments in renewable energy, no to renewable fuels. And today, we import triple the amount of oil as the day that Senator McCain took office.

Now is the time to end this addiction, and to understand that drilling is a stopgap measure, not a long-term solution. Not even close.

As president, I will tap our natural gas reserves, invest in clean coal technology, and find ways to safely harness nuclear power. I'll help our auto companies retool, so that the fuel-efficient cars of the future are built right here in America. I'll make it easier for the American people to afford these new cars. And I'll invest $150 billion over the next decade in affordable, renewable sources of energy - wind power and solar power and the next generation of biofuels; an investment that will lead to new industries and 5 million new jobs that pay well and can't ever be outsourced.

America, now is not the time for small plans.

Now is the time to finally meet our moral obligation to provide every child a world-class education, because it will take nothing less to compete in the global economy. Michelle and I are only here tonight because we were given a chance at an education. And I will not settle for an America where some kids don't have that chance. I'll invest in early childhood education. I'll recruit an army of new teachers, and pay them higher salaries and give them more support. And in exchange, I'll ask for higher standards and more accountability. And we will keep our promise to every young American - if you commit to serving your community or your country, we will make sure you can afford a college education.

Now is the time to finally keep the promise of affordable, accessible health care for every single American. If you have health care, my plan will lower your premiums. If you don't, you'll be able to get the same kind of coverage that members of Congress give themselves. And as someone who watched my mother argue with insurance companies while she lay in bed dying of cancer, I will make certain those companies stop discriminating against those who are sick and need care the most.

Now is the time to help families with paid sick days and better family leave, because nobody in America should have to choose between keeping their jobs and caring for a sick child or ailing parent.

Now is the time to change our bankruptcy laws, so that your pensions are protected ahead of CEO bonuses; and the time to protect Social Security for future generations.

And now is the time to keep the promise of equal pay for an equal day's work, because I want my daughters to have exactly the same opportunities as your sons.

Now, many of these plans will cost money, which is why I've laid out how I'll pay for every dime - by closing corporate loopholes and tax havens that don't help America grow. But I will also go through the federal budget, line by line, eliminating programs that no longer work and making the ones we do need work better and cost less - because we cannot meet twenty-first-century challenges with a twentieth-century bureaucracy.

And Democrats, we must also admit that fulfilling America's promise will require more than just money. It will require a renewed sense of responsibility from each of us to recover what John F. Kennedy called our "intellectual and moral strength." Yes, government must lead on energy independence, but each of us must do our part to make our homes and businesses more efficient. Yes, we must provide more ladders to success for young men who fall into lives of crime and despair. But we must also admit that programs alone can't replace parents; that government can't turn off the television and make a child do her homework; that fathers must take more responsibility for providing the love and guidance their children need.

Individual responsibility and mutual responsibility - that's the essence of America's promise.

And just as we keep our promise to the next generation here at home, so must we keep America's promise abroad. If John McCain wants to have a debate about who has the temperament, and judgment, to serve as the next commander in chief, that's a debate I'm ready to have.

For while Senator McCain was turning his sights to Iraq just days after 9/11, I stood up and opposed this war, knowing that it would distract us from the real threats we face. When John McCain said we could just "muddle through" in Afghanistan, I argued for more resources and more troops to finish the fight against the terrorists who actually attacked us on 9/11, and made clear that we must take out Osama bin Laden and his lieutenants if we have them in our sights. John McCain likes to say that he'll follow bin Laden to the gates of hell - but he won't even go to the cave where he lives.

And today, as my call for a time frame to remove our troops from Iraq has been echoed by the Iraqi government and even the Bush administration, even after we learned that Iraq has a $79 billion surplus while we're wallowing in deficits, John McCain stands alone in his stubborn refusal to end a misguided war.

That's not the judgment we need. That won't keep America safe. We need a president who can face the threats of the future, not keep grasping at the ideas of the past.

You don't defeat a terrorist network that operates in 80 countries by occupying Iraq. You don't protect Israel and deter Iran just by talking tough in Washington. You can't truly stand up for Georgia when you've strained our oldest alliances. If John McCain wants to follow George Bush with more tough talk and bad strategy, that is his choice - but it is not the change we need.

We are the party of Roosevelt. We are the party of Kennedy. So don't tell me that Democrats won't defend this country. Don't tell me that Democrats won't keep us safe. The Bush–McCain foreign policy has squandered the legacy that generations of Americans - Democrats and Republicans - have built, and we are here to restore that legacy.

As commander in chief, I will never hesitate to defend this nation, but I will only send our troops into harm's way with a clear mission and a sacred commitment to give them the equipment they need in battle and the care and benefits they deserve when they come home.

I will end this war in Iraq responsibly, and finish the fight against Al Qaeda and the Taliban in Afghanistan. I will rebuild our military to meet future conflicts. But I will also renew the tough, direct diplomacy that can prevent Iran from obtaining nuclear weapons and curb Russian aggression. I will build new partnerships to defeat the threats of the twenty-first century: terrorism and nuclear proliferation; poverty and genocide; climate change and disease. And I will restore our moral standing, so that America is once again that last, best hope for all who are called to the cause of freedom, who long for lives of peace, and who yearn for a better future.

These are the policies I will pursue. And in the weeks ahead, I look forward to debating them with John McCain.

But what I will not do is suggest that the senator takes his positions for political purposes. Because one of the things that we have to change in our politics is the idea that people cannot disagree without challenging each other's character and patriotism.

The times are too serious, the stakes are too high for this same partisan playbook. So let us agree that patriotism has no party. I love this country, and so do you, and so does John McCain. The men and women who serve in our battlefields may be Democrats and Republicans and Independents, but they have fought together and bled together and some died together under the same proud flag. They have not served a Red America or a Blue America - they have served the United States of America.

So I've got news for you, John McCain. We all put our country first.

America, our work will not be easy. The challenges we face require tough choices, and Democrats as well as Republicans will need to cast off the worn-out ideas and politics of the past. For part of what has been lost these past eight years can't just be measured by lost wages or bigger trade deficits. What has also been lost is our sense of common purpose - our sense of higher purpose. And that's what we have to restore.

We may not agree on abortion, but surely we can agree on reducing the number of unwanted pregnancies in this country. The reality of gun ownership may be different for hunters in rural Ohio than for those plagued by gang violence in Cleveland, but don't tell me we can't uphold the Second Amendment while keeping AK-47s out of the hands of criminals. I know there are differences on same-sex marriage, but surely we can agree that our gay and lesbian brothers and sisters deserve to visit the person they love in the hospital and to live lives free of discrimination. Passions fly on immigration, but I don't know anyone who benefits when a mother is separated from her infant child or an employer undercuts American wages by hiring illegal workers. This too is part of America's promise - the promise of a democracy where we can find the strength and grace to bridge divides and unite in common effort.

I know there are those who dismiss such beliefs as happy talk. They claim that our insistence on something larger, something firmer and more honest in our public life is just a Trojan Horse for higher taxes and the abandonment of traditional values. And that's to be expected. Because if you don't have any fresh ideas, then you use stale tactics to scare the voters. If you don't have a record to run on, then you paint your opponent as someone people should run from.

You make a big election about small things.

And you know what - it's worked before. Because it feeds into the cynicism we all have about government. When Washington doesn't work, all its promises seem empty. If your hopes have been dashed again and again, then it's best to stop hoping, and settle for what you already know.

I get it. I realize that I am not the likeliest candidate for this office. I don't fit the typical pedigree, and I haven't spent my career in the halls of Washington.

But I stand before you tonight because all across America something is stirring. What the naysayers don't understand is that this election has never been about me. It's been about you.

For 18 long months, you have stood up, one by one, and said enough to the politics of the past. You understand that in this election, the greatest risk we can take is to try the same old politics with the same old players and expect a different result. You have shown what history teaches us - that at defining moments like this one, the change we need doesn't come from Washington. Change comes to Washington. Change happens because the American people demand it - because they rise up and insist on new ideas and new leadership, a new politics for a new time.

America, this is one of those moments.

I believe that as hard as it will be, the change we need is coming. Because I've seen it. Because I've lived it. I've seen it in Illinois, when we provided health care to more children and moved more families from welfare to work. I've seen it in Washington, when we worked across party lines to open up government and hold lobbyists more accountable, to give better care for our veterans and keep nuclear weapons out of terrorist hands.

And I've seen it in this campaign. In the young people who voted for the first time, and in those who got involved again after a very long time. In the Republicans who never thought they'd pick up a Democratic ballot, but did. I've seen it in the workers who would rather cut their hours back a day than see their friends lose their jobs, in the soldiers who reenlist after losing a limb, in the good neighbors who take a stranger in when a hurricane strikes and the floodwaters rise.

This country of ours has more wealth than any nation, but that's not what makes us rich. We have the most powerful military on earth, but that's not what makes us strong. Our universities and our culture are the envy of the world, but that's not what keeps the world coming to our shores.

Instead, it is that American spirit - that American promise - that pushes us forward even when the path is uncertain; that binds us together in spite of our differences; that makes us fix our eye not on what is seen, but what is unseen, that better place around the bend.

That promise is our greatest inheritance. It's a promise I make to my daughters when I tuck them in at night, and a promise that you make to yours - a promise that has led immigrants to cross oceans and pioneers to travel west; a promise that led workers to picket lines and women to reach for the ballot.

And it is that promise that 45 years ago today brought Americans from every corner of this land to stand together on a mall in Washington, before Lincoln's Memorial, and hear a young preacher from Georgia speak of his dream.

The men and women who gathered there could've heard many things. They could've heard words of anger and discord. They could've been told to succumb to the fear and frustration of so many dreams deferred.

But what the people heard instead - people of every creed and color, from every walk of life - is that in America, our destiny is inextricably linked. That together, our dreams can be one.

"We cannot walk alone," the preacher cried. "And as we walk, we must make the pledge that we shall always march ahead. We cannot turn back."

America, we cannot turn back. Not with so much work to be done. Not with so many children to educate, and so many veterans to care for. Not with an economy to fix and cities to rebuild and farms to save. Not with so many families to protect and so many lives to mend. America, we cannot turn back. We cannot walk alone. At this moment, in this election, we must pledge once more to march into the future. Let us keep that promise - that American promise - and, in the words of Scripture, hold firmly, without wavering, to the hope that we confess.

Thank you.

God bless you. And God bless the United States of America.

CHANGE
WE NEED

@ WWW.BARACKOBAMA.COM

PAID FOR BY OBAMA FOR AMERICA

CHANGE WE NEED

⬤ WWW.BARACKOBAMA.COM

Supporters express
a range of deeply felt
emotions as Barack
speaks at a rally
in Miami, Florida,
October 21, 2008.

The family walks onstage the last night of the Democratic National Convention at Invesco Field in Denver, August 28, 2008.

THE PERFECT STORM

The story will be told for generations: A Black man—elegant in his appearance, brilliant in his delivery—beat out the toughest politicians in the nation to become the first Black American president. Reporting from the venerable Ebenezer Baptist Church in Atlanta, ISABEL WILKERSON, *the Pulitzer Prize-winning journalist, combed through the data to tell us just how the race was won*

Tuesday, *November 4, 2008,*
7:00 P.M. (EST)

A few polls had just closed on the East Coast. Crowds had already gathered on both sides of Auburn Avenue, where Martin Luther King, Jr., had led the Civil Rights Movement from Atlanta. The throng filled the sidewalks and the lawn of Ebenezer Baptist Church, a bittersweet warrior of a church, one of the most famous in America.

The people stood holding candles, so many candles that all that could be seen was a sea of blinking diamonds in the velvet night. There was no room to move and too many people to fit into the sanctuary. There was an uncharacteristic air of oneness, of letting others go ahead of you, of making room for fathers with strollers and elders with canes, of smiling into the eyes of the person beside you. The crowd was silent, as if holding its collective breath after so many months of being on the verge of the impossible.

The numbers began coming in. The people scrolled their BlackBerrys and strained to hear on their cell phones. Vermont had been called for Senator Barack Obama of Illinois. New Jersey, Connecticut, Massachusetts. But they were expected. The electoral votes were already looking lopsided in Obama's favor.

Then someone shouted, "He won Pennsylvania!" as if she herself had won Pennsylvania, which in a way, she had. The texting sped up, grew more urgent and frenetic. The crowd began to sense change in the wind. People too young to remember the movement began singing spirituals and movement songs from the sixties: "This little light of

Obama waves to the crowd at a rally in the rain at the University of Mary Washington in Fredericksburg, Virginia, September 27, 2008.

mine, I'm going to let it shine. Let it shine. Let it shine. Let it shine...."

At the side of the church, clumps of people who couldn't get inside stood on their tiptoes, their faces pressed against the sanctuary windows. They held their cameras to the windows and craned to see the election results on the screens inside. "He won Ohio!" a woman reported to the people around her. "We're leading Florida. It's real. Oh, God!"

The Day Before Tomorrow

By 11:00 P.M. (EST), at the precise moment the polls closed on the West Coast, the race was over, stunning in its speed and finality. That night, for the first time in history, in a country where Blacks were long prohibited from voting at all, an African-American was elected president of the United States. It will take time to digest that statement. Generations from now history books will record the election, and children will tell their grandchildren about the night a Black man won the highest office in the land. But that doesn't begin to capture the significance and meaning of the election we had just witnessed.

How he won is perhaps as extraordinary as the winning itself. His biography is well-known by now: only son of a Kenyan father and a White mother from Kansas who met in Hawaii, Columbia undergrad, Harvard Law and so on. But what will take time to absorb is how a Black man, a virtually unknown state senator from Illinois, fast-forwarded past more obstacles than one dares contemplate to make it to the White House.

So many things that could have gone wrong didn't. So many things he did were absolutely on target. So many things beyond anyone's control went in his favor—the credit crisis, the gas crisis, the Wall Street meltdown, the stock market bust. At every turn, so many things had to happen to make the unthinkable possible that it required the perfect storm of a flawless campaign, an inspiring and disciplined candidate, an electorate hungry for his message, the foibles and missteps of his opponents and an economy in such turmoil that even people who never thought they would vote for a Black man felt they had no choice.

It could be said that the first stirrings began when Obama won the Democratic nomination for the U.S. Senate from Illinois. His Republican opponent got caught in a sex scandal and had to drop out. Obama was tapped to deliver a speech at the 2004 Democratic National Convention. Had he not given that career-defining speech, the buzz might not have spread that he could be a presidential contender. Without the buzz, he might not have gotten support early enough to mount a strong campaign, and so on. He had the impeccable timing of running when the incumbent President, George W. Bush, had the lowest approval ratings of any president in modern history, when gas prices were the highest recorded, when the stock market plunged dramatically in the past year, when banks were collapsing and we were in the midst of two intractable and unpopular wars. Add to that an uncharacteristically disorganized Republican opponent with an offbeat running mate more visible on *Saturday Night Live* than on the sober Sunday morning news shows, and Barack Obama had his perfect storm.

The Game Changer

It seems inevitable now. But for months, the press and the pundits fretted over the role of race in the campaign, focusing first on whether he was Black enough to get Black support, then whether he was mainstream enough to get White votes, then whether the polls showing the race tightening or loosening were accurate, and then whether the undecided voters were McCain supporters in hiding who might sink Obama's ambitions.

Throughout the obsessing, Obama plowed through red states and blue states, seeming to pay the hand-wringing no mind, running what even his opponents described as a near-flawless campaign. It was a millennial, technocratic, Internet-powered grassroots movement that virtually willed a voter base by inviting people to donate as little as $5, asking them to recruit a friend to do the same, flooding them with e-mail updates on Obama's every move and then, most important, directing them to the nearest polls by ZIP code on November 4. The campaign built its own voter bloc, and thus came victory, the way sleeper movies become blockbusters, through momentum and word of mouth. And that was just the ground game.

The candidate himself was not just a Black candidate with Black support, as television pundits often portrayed him to be, particularly during the Democratic primaries, where it was said he might not do well in this or that state because the Black vote was only approximately 13 percent of the total U.S. population. How quickly some in the press forgot that he won the Iowa caucuses over the formidable front-runner and most famous woman in politics, Hillary Clinton, and over the former vice-presidential candidate John Edwards, both of whom had deeply loyal fan bases in a state that was close to 95 percent White.

What made him distinctive was not his race but the machine-like discipline of an Ivy League professorial overachiever, who seemed able to tap into the frustrations of an electorate, a country that was fed up with an exceptionally unpopular incumbent and looking for something to believe in. He managed to maintain his cool regardless of the circumstances, and seemed never to need sleep. Steve Schmidt, chief strategist for his opponent John McCain, quoted in *The New York Times*, described Obama as a formidable candidate, "ice-cold disciplined about the execution of his campaign message."

Breaking Many Barriers

November 2, 2008. Ebenezer Baptist Church, Atlanta. It was the Sunday before Election Day. A calm had settled over the sanctuary. All that could be done had been done. It was now in God's hands.

A simple wooden cross hung from the skylit ceiling, as the pastor, the Reverend Raphael G. Warnock, began to pray. "We pray for the morning," he intoned. "We pray for the nation at this time of transition as we go to the polls. Hear our prayers, oh, God." He looked out at the packed pews and asked how many people had already voted. Nearly every hand went up.

"Amen," he said in approval.

Throughout the service, he did not call Obama by name. It was bigger than him. This was the church of Dr. King and so many others who had not lived to see this day. It was as if it was understood that the dream was so close, it dared not be uttered.

"We are on the brink of a promise," the reverend said.

It could not have been known then, but Barack Obama was not just about to win. He was about to break records in a way that Democrats, so accustomed to heartbreaking squeakers that came down to one battleground state, could not have fathomed going in. The campaign will likely be studied by politicians and strategists for many election cycles to come. What does it take, they will ask, for an African-American with an unusual last name, no political pedigree, from a battered political party that had lost its hold on a whole section of the country (the South) and had lost more than half of all presidential elections since the 1950's—

Obama gives the Stars and Stripes new meaning at a rally in Canton, Ohio, a week before the election.

what does it take for such a candidate to win?

The extraordinary nature of Obama's win on that Tuesday in November only begins with his race. Since 1960, when John F. Kennedy eked out a victory over Richard M. Nixon, no Democrat has won the White House unless he was from the South. Until that Tuesday. In the past 40 years, only two Democrats have made it to the White House, and they were both southern governors whose last names began with the letter *C* (Jimmy Carter and Bill Clinton). Until that Tuesday. No Democrat had won the states of Virginia and Indiana since Johnson. Until that Tuesday.

Obama was the first to win North Carolina since Jimmy Carter; North Carolina having eluded the more popular fellow southerner Bill Clinton. Indeed, Obama won states that were inconceivable just four years ago, handily carrying the two that had ended the hopes of Al Gore in 2000 (Florida) and John Kerry in 2004 (Ohio), winning with large enough margins that there was no need for talk of hanging chads or recounts. Obama broke all kinds of records—more people watched CNN that night than any night in its history; more text messages were sent between 11:00 P.M. and midnight than ever before—and nearly every kernel of conventional wisdom. He was not a governor, as most presidents in modern times of any party have been. His name does not end with a consonant, which was a long-held axiom of the presidency. Until that Tuesday.

He virtually rewrote the rules of campaign fund-raising in ways that candidates will likely seek to emulate in elections to come. The campaign raised some $640 million, that is, nearly two thirds of a billion dollars—more than any candidate in U.S. presidential history. Perhaps most surprising, Obama literally did what no one who has ever run for president has done: More Americans voted for him than for anyone who has ever run for the top job. He won 66,760,924 popular votes—more than George W. Bush, who ran with the advantage of incumbency in 2004 (62,028,285 votes), more than Bill Clinton in his 1996 reelection (47,402,357 votes), and even more than the president who won by a landslide, Ronald Reagan, in 1984

(54,455,075 votes). The nation's population has grown since the days of Reagan, but the numbers are breathtaking given the unlikely odds facing an unknown politician who just four years ago was a fairly new state senator in Illinois.

Thus, while much of the coverage has focused on the meaning of his victory to Black voters, that emphasis does not acknowledge the candidate's disciplined strategy, the multiracial nature of his campaign, the many famous and unknown people who gave their lives so that Black people might be in a position to run for the highest office, and the deepest wishes of many African-Americans who held their breaths in hopes that their fellow Americans of other colors might support someone who looked like them.

The momentous nature of his win extends to the composition of those who voted for him. The truth of the matter is that, like other Democrats, Obama could not have won the election without the Black vote. But while Black voters turned out in droves for him, he could not have won on the basis of the Black vote alone. And, like other Democrats, if he had had to depend on the White vote alone, as *The New York Times* observed, he would have lost. Still, despite worries about what White voters might or might not do, it appears that Obama did better than most Democratic nominees. The average Democrat running for president draws 39 percent of the White vote, according to a *New York Times*/CBS News poll. Data showed Obama drawing 44 percent support among Whites, a higher percentage than Bill Clinton.

Obama, by his charisma, the devotion of his tear-filled fans, the massive multiracial crowds he drew, the global obsession with his victory and the virtual movement he created, may have already secured a place for himself among figures such as Martin Luther King, Jr., and Nelson Mandela. But it will take time to digest the many other points of significance of a once little-known state legislator leading a moribund political party to a decisive and long-awaited victory with the votes of so many inspired people of every color, age and creed.

Ebenezer Baptist Church, Postelection Sunday

"We will tell the coming generations of the glorious deeds of the Lord," Rev. Warnock is saying to a packed house of parishioners who appear to be walking more lightly, backs straighter, with smiles they can't contain. "How many of you know that the Lord is still good?" he asked the congregation to a chorus of "Yes, Lords" and "Amens."

Then he mentioned the president-elect by name. "Barack Obama stood this week against the fierce tide of history and achieved the unimaginable," he said. "But he didn't get where he is by himself. And wherever he is, you stand there, too. Somebody had to pay a mighty high price for you to sit where you sit and stand where you stand."

He named Dr. King, Medgar Evers, Fannie Lou Hamer, Septima Clark, Shirley Chisholm, Jesse Jackson and others who led the way or "planted the seed of the unimaginable in the imagination of the American people."

John Lewis, the congressman and foot soldier of the movement who attends Ebenezer, testified: "This is the most powerful moment in modern American history. It's the beginning of a new beginning. I feel blessed to be living. But I'm sad that so many people who began on this journey didn't live to see it. Some shot, some lynched, some beaten. Some never got to vote at all. We voted for them. We voted for them."

This article first appeared in the January 2009 issue of ESSENCE.

Thousands gather in New York City's Times Square on Election Night just after the historic win.

"THIS IS OUR MOMENT"

On November 4, 2008, Barack Obama celebrated his historic victory as the first African-American president of the United States of America in Chicago's Grant Park. He spoke just before midnight EST, signaling a new direction for our nation and the world

I f there is anyone out there who still doubts that America is a place where all things are possible; who still wonders if the dream of our founders is alive in our time; who still questions the power of our democracy, tonight is your answer.

It's the answer told by lines that stretched around schools and churches in numbers this nation has never seen; by people who waited three hours and four hours, many for the very first time in their lives, because they believed that this time must be different; that their voice could be that difference.

It's the answer spoken by young and old, rich and poor, Democrat and Republican, black, white, Latino, Asian, Native American, gay, straight, disabled and not disabled - Americans who sent a message to the world that we have never been a collection of Red States and Blue States: We are, and always will be, the United States of America.

It's the answer that led those who have been told for so long by so many to be cynical, and fearful, and doubtful of what we can achieve to put their hands on the arc of history and bend it once more toward the hope of a better day.

It's been a long time coming, but tonight, because of what we did on this day, in this election, at this defining moment, change has come to America.

I just received a very gracious call from Senator McCain. He fought long and hard in this campaign, and he's fought even longer and harder for the country he loves. He has endured sacrifices for America that most of us cannot begin to imagine, and we are better off for the service rendered by this brave and selfless leader. I congratulate him and Governor Palin for all they have achieved, and I look forward to working with them to renew this nation's promise in the months ahead.

I want to thank my partner in this journey, a man who campaigned from his heart and spoke for the men and women he grew up with on the streets of Scranton and rode with on that train home to Delaware, the Vice President-elect of the United States, Joe Biden.

I would not be standing here tonight without the unyielding support of my best friend for the last 16 years, the rock of our family and the love of my life, our nation's next First Lady, Michelle Obama. Sasha and Malia, I love you both so much, and you have earned the new puppy that's coming with us to the White House. And while she's no longer with us, I know my grandmother is watching, along with the family that made me who I am. I miss them tonight, and know that my debt to them is beyond measure.

Obama and his family rejoice in their hometown after his unprecedented triumph in the national election.

To my campaign manager David Plouffe, my chief strategist David Axelrod, and the best campaign team ever assembled in the history of politics - you made this happen, and I am forever grateful for what you've sacrificed to get it done.

But above all, I will never forget who this victory truly belongs to - it belongs to you.

I was never the likeliest candidate for this office. We didn't start with much money or many endorsements. Our campaign was not hatched in the halls of Washington - it began in the backyards of Des Moines and the living rooms of Concord and the front porches of Charleston.

It was built by working men and women who dug into what little savings they had to give $5 and $10 and $20 to this cause. It grew strength from the young people who rejected the myth of their generation's apathy; who left their homes and their families for jobs that offered little pay and less sleep; from the not-so-young people who braved the bitter cold and scorching heat to knock on the doors of perfect strangers; from the millions of Americans who volunteered, and organized, and proved that more than two centuries later, a government of the people, by the people and for the people has not perished from this earth. This is your victory.

I know you didn't do this just to win an election and I know you didn't do it for me. You did it because you understand the enormity of the task that lies ahead. For even as we celebrate tonight, we know the challenges that tomorrow will bring are the greatest of our lifetime - two wars, a planet in peril, the worst financial crisis in a century. Even as we stand here tonight, we know there are brave Americans waking up in the deserts of Iraq and the mountains of Afghanistan to risk their lives for us. There are mothers and fathers who will lie awake after their children fall asleep and wonder how they'll make the mortgage, or pay their doctor's bills, or save enough for college. There is new energy to harness and new jobs to be created; new schools to build and threats to meet and alliances to repair.

The road ahead will be long. Our climb will be steep. We may not get there in one year or even one term, but America - I have never been more hopeful than I am tonight that we will get there. I promise you - we as a people will get there.

There will be setbacks and false starts. There are many who won't agree with every decision or policy I make as president, and we know that government can't solve every problem. But I will always be honest with you about the challenges we face. I will listen to you, especially when we disagree. And above all, I will ask you to join in the work of remaking this nation the only way it's been done in America for 221 years; block by block, brick by brick, calloused hand by calloused hand.

What began 21 months ago in the depths of winter must not end on this autumn night. This victory alone is not the change we seek - it is only the chance for us to make that change. And that cannot happen if we go back to the way things were. It cannot happen without you.

So let us summon a new spirit of patriotism; of service and responsibility where each of us resolves to pitch in and work harder and look after not only ourselves, but each other. Let us remember that if this financial crisis taught us anything, it's that we cannot have a thriving Wall Street while Main Street suffers - in this country, we rise or fall as one nation; as one people.

Let us resist the temptation to fall back on the same partisanship and pettiness and immaturity that has poisoned our politics for so long. Let us remember that it was a man from this state who first carried the banner of the Republican Party to the White House - a party founded on the values of self-reliance, individual liberty, and national unity. Those are values we all share, and while the Democratic Party has won a great victory tonight, we do so with a measure of humility and determination to heal the divides that have held back our progress. As Lincoln said to a nation far more divided than ours, "We are not enemies, but friends...though passion may have strained, it must not break our bonds of affection." And to those Americans whose support I have yet to earn - I may not have won your vote, but I hear your voices, I need your help, and I will be your president too.

And to all those watching tonight from beyond our shores, from parliaments and palaces to those who are huddled around radios in the forgotten corners of our world - our stories are singular, but our destiny is shared, and a new dawn of American leadership is at hand. To those who would tear this world down - we will defeat you. To those who seek peace and security - we support you. And to all those who have wondered if America's beacon still burns as bright - tonight we proved once more that the true strength of our nation comes not from the might of our arms or the scale of our wealth, but from the enduring power of our ideals: democracy, liberty, opportunity, and unyielding hope.

For that is the true genius of America - that America can change. Our union can be perfected. And what we have already achieved gives us hope for what we can and must achieve tomorrow.

This election had many firsts and many stories that will be told for generations. But one that's on my mind tonight is about a woman who cast her ballot in Atlanta. She's a lot like the millions of others who stood in line to make their voice heard in this election except for one thing - Ann Nixon Cooper is 106 years old.

She was born just a generation past slavery; a time when there were no cars on the road or planes in the sky; when someone like her couldn't vote for two reasons - because she was a woman and because of the color of her skin.

And tonight, I think about all that she's seen throughout her century in America - the heartache and the hope; the struggle and the progress; the times we were told that we can't, and the people who pressed on with that American creed: Yes we can.

At a time when women's voices were silenced and their hopes dismissed, she lived to see them stand up and speak out and reach for the ballot. Yes we can.

When there was despair in the dust bowl and depression across the land, she saw a nation conquer fear itself with a New Deal, new jobs and a new sense of common purpose. Yes we can.

When the bombs fell on our harbor and tyranny threatened the world, she was there to witness a generation rise to greatness and a democracy was saved. Yes we can.

She was there for the buses in Montgomery, the hoses in Birmingham, a bridge in Selma, and a preacher from Atlanta who told a people that "We Shall Overcome." Yes we can.

A man touched down on the moon, a wall came down in Berlin, a world was connected by our own science and imagination. And this year, in this election, she touched her finger to a screen, and cast her vote, because after 106 years in America, through the best of times and the darkest of hours, she knows how America can change. Yes we can.

America, we have come so far. We have seen so much. But there is so much more to do. So tonight, let us ask ourselves - if our children should live to see the next century; if my daughters should be so lucky to live as long as Ann Nixon Cooper, what change will they see? What progress will we have made?

This is our chance to answer that call. This is our moment. This is our time - to put our people back to work and open doors of opportunity for our kids; to restore prosperity and promote the cause of peace; to reclaim the American Dream and reaffirm that fundamental truth - that out of many, we are one; that while we breathe, we hope, and where we are met with cynicism, and doubt, and those who tell us that we can't, we will respond with that timeless creed that sums up the spirit of a people: Yes we can.

Thank you. God bless you, and may God bless the United States of America.

Part 3

WHAT THEY MEAN TO US

Our dreams about the future of the Black family
had been nearly extinguished—now the fires of hope
burn bright. They represent the best of who we are. They're
the graceful family we see in church. They inspire us
with their family values. Their extended family tree of
grandparents, siblings, cousins and friends remind us
of our powerful familial bonds. And they assure us of our
endless and extraordinary possibilities.

———

Why I Voted

DANA ROXETTE
Atlanta

When I arrived at the voting center at 6 A.M., I felt voting was something I had to do for myself and others around me. The young people who were voting for the first time and the volunteers, who were eager to sign us up and get us voting, were inspirational. But when I stepped into that booth, it became spiritual to me. Anything in God's power is possible. I said a small prayer that this election be in His hands and His will be done.

An eager crowd
awaits Michelle
at a Get Out
the Vote rally in
Los Angeles,
February 3, 2008.

This page: At home on MLK Drive in southwest Atlanta the day after the election, Ann Nixon Cooper, with pictures spread in front of her, talks about the victory she never thought she would see in her lifetime. Opposite page: This framed photo of young Ann Nixon Cooper hangs in her living room.

REFLECTIONS OF A 107-YEAR-OLD VOTER

Ann Nixon Cooper has seen a lot in her more than one hundred years, and one of her greatest moments occurred on November 4, when she voted for Barack Obama

By Wendy L. Wilson

"Just like Martin, we're all hoping that he'll make things easier," says 107-year-old Ann Louise Nixon Cooper, who sees similarities between Dr. Martin Luther King, Jr., and the man who will be our forty-fourth president. "There will always be a connection between them." She remembers spending days with his mother, Alberta Williams King.

The history maker, President Barack Obama, made Ann Nixon Cooper a legend when he specifically thanked her in his acceptance speech at Grant Park in Chicago:

"This election had many firsts and many stories that will be told for generations," he said. "But one that's on my mind tonight is about a woman who cast her ballot in Atlanta. She's a lot like the millions of others who stood in line to make their voice heard in this election except for one thing: Ann Nixon Cooper is 106 years old.

"She was born just a generation past slavery; a time when there were no cars on the road or planes in the sky; when someone like her couldn't vote for two reasons: because she was a woman and because of the color of her skin.

"She was there for the buses in Montgomery, the hoses in Birmingham, a bridge in Selma and a preacher from Atlanta who told a people that 'We Shall Overcome.' Yes we can.

"A man touched down on the moon, a wall came down in Berlin, a world was connected by our own science and imagination. And this year, in this election, she touched her finger to a screen and cast her vote, because after 106 years in America, through the best of times and the darkest of hours, she knows how America can change. Yes we can."

"It's just great!" Nixon Cooper says of the publicity she's received. "I may be sitting in my chair but there is always something on my mind."

"We've all forgotten those days," she says, not wishing to focus on the struggles so many men and women encountered to obtain the right to vote. While she doesn't remember the first time she went to polls, she does remember she was "good and grown." Nixon Cooper would have been 63 years old when the Voting Rights Act was passed in 1965, guaranteeing African-Americans the right to cast the ballot.

Born Ann Louise Nixon in Shelbyville, Tennessee, on January 9, 1902, Nixon Cooper was one of eight children in her family. She married Albert Cooper, a prominent dentist, in 1922, when she was just 20 years old. They moved to Atlanta and started a family. Nixon Cooper was involved in the Civil Rights Movement and has always given back to the community, having cofounded a Girls' Club for African-American youth and teaching people to read in a tutoring program at Ebenezer Baptist Church.

Nixon Cooper voted for Obama because "he offered the most different things for us...things that no one else had."

An excerpt of this article first appeared November 5, 2008, on Essence.com.

Why I Voted

ERIN BAILEY
Maryland

I was in line by 6:55 A.M. I was so excited to see hundreds of people in my community standing in line. I just couldn't believe it. I went in and voted. At 8:05, I raced out of the polls and created a video to let everyone know exactly how I felt. I am so ridiculously proud of my country and all the people who voted!

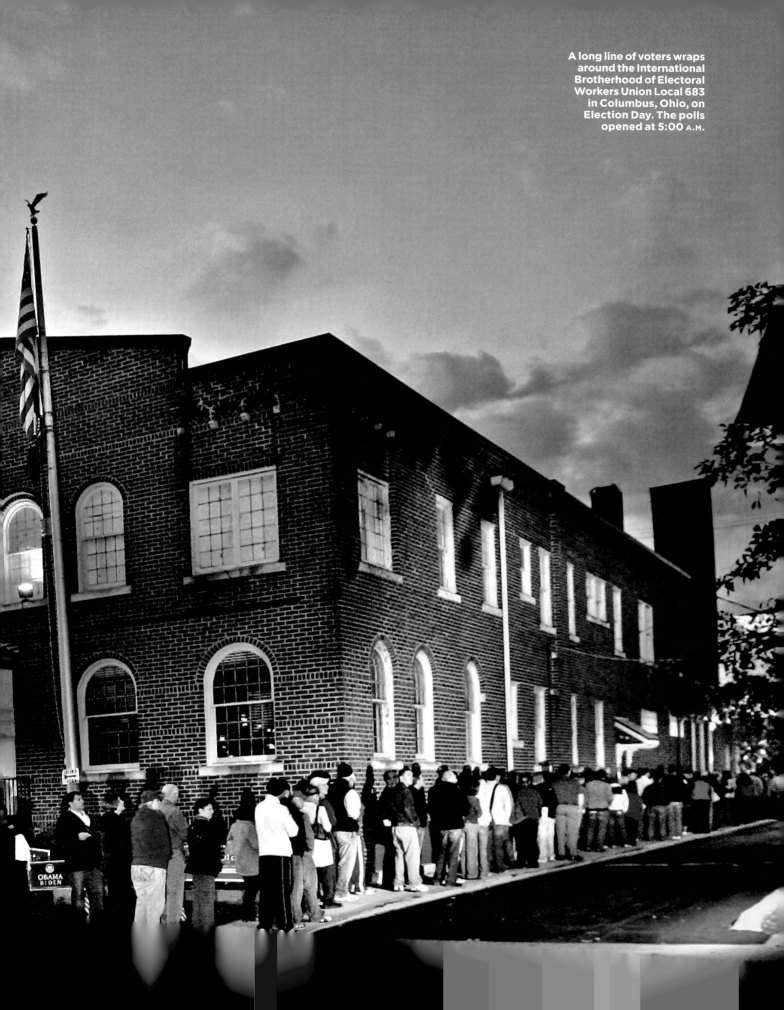

A long line of voters wraps around the International Brotherhood of Electoral Workers Union Local 683 in Columbus, Ohio, on Election Day. The polls opened at 5:00 A.M.

—

Why I Voted

NANCY FITZPATRICK
Montgomery, Alabama

Before 8 A.M., there were cars parked on both sides of four highway lanes for almost two miles— unusual for this small, southern Black community. The elderly were standing on walkers and sitting on chairs in line to participate in the event they never thought would occur in their lifetimes. They had registered to vote during a time when they knew it would bring racial persecution against them and their families. Yet bravely they stood in the belief that their press toward the mark of the liberation of the Black race would bring forth triumph. And indeed, that belief reverberated as I witnessed these soldiers press, yet again, across four lanes of highway on walkers and canes and in wheelchairs to do their duty once more. It was a walk around the walls of Jericho for the future of Black folks in America. One 80-year-old lady refused a chair. She was determined to stand until she was able to cast her vote. Another woman just shook her head and wept while she waited in line. I felt my heart swell as I watched my fathers dare to beam with pride. They stood a little taller while they waited their turn to cast their ballot.

A voter uses
a magnifying glass
to read his ballot
at a polling station
in Chicago.

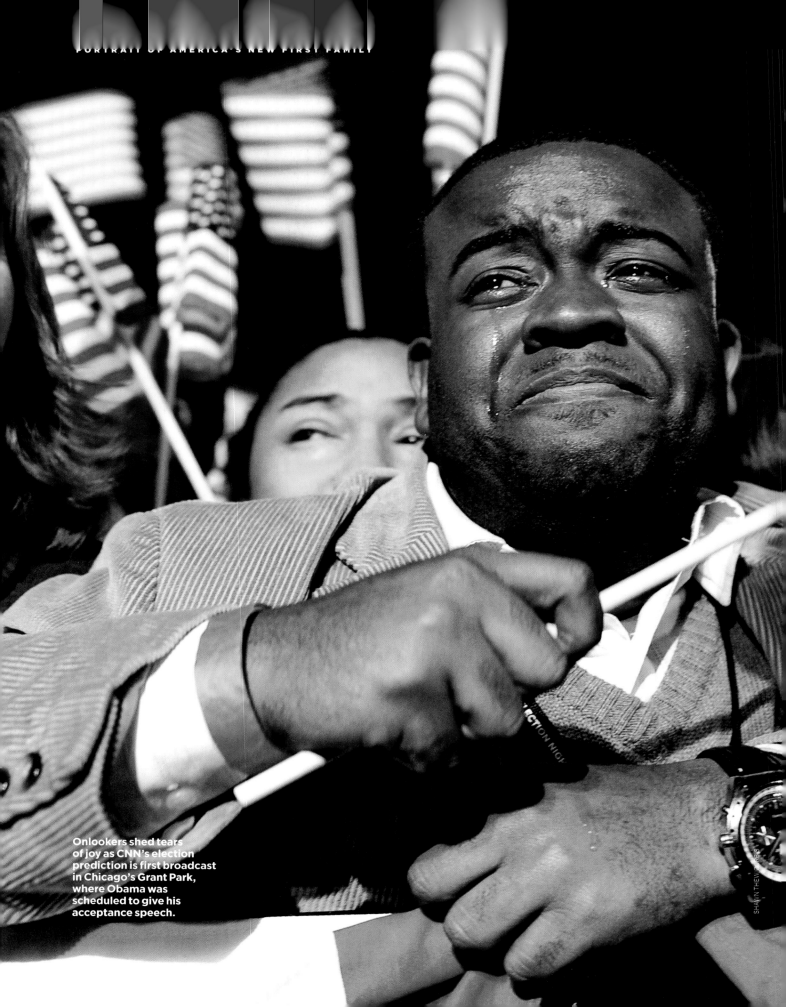

Onlookers shed tears of joy as CNN's election prediction is first broadcast in Chicago's Grant Park, where Obama was scheduled to give his acceptance speech.

Why I Voted

KATHY JOHNSON
Columbus/Fort Benning, Georgia

I sit in awe of what the Lord has allowed to manifest today. I am a military soldier with 24 years of active duty who retired three months ago. I was at the polling location at 5:30 A.M. It was an inspiration to see the vast turnout of African-American voters. It was an emotional blessing to see the older generation move to the front of the line to vote. Then it really hit me that I was voting for many purposes. I was representing myself as a recently retired soldier who for the first time was not overseas serving my country and casting an absentee ballot. I was voting in person for the first time. I was voting for all my military comrades who made the supreme sacrifice and could not know this historical election— the first African-American male for president, and the first female for vice-president. I was voting for my mother, grandmother and great-grandmother, who did not live to experience this history being made. If I wasn't proud and tearful! Truly, today is a blessing.

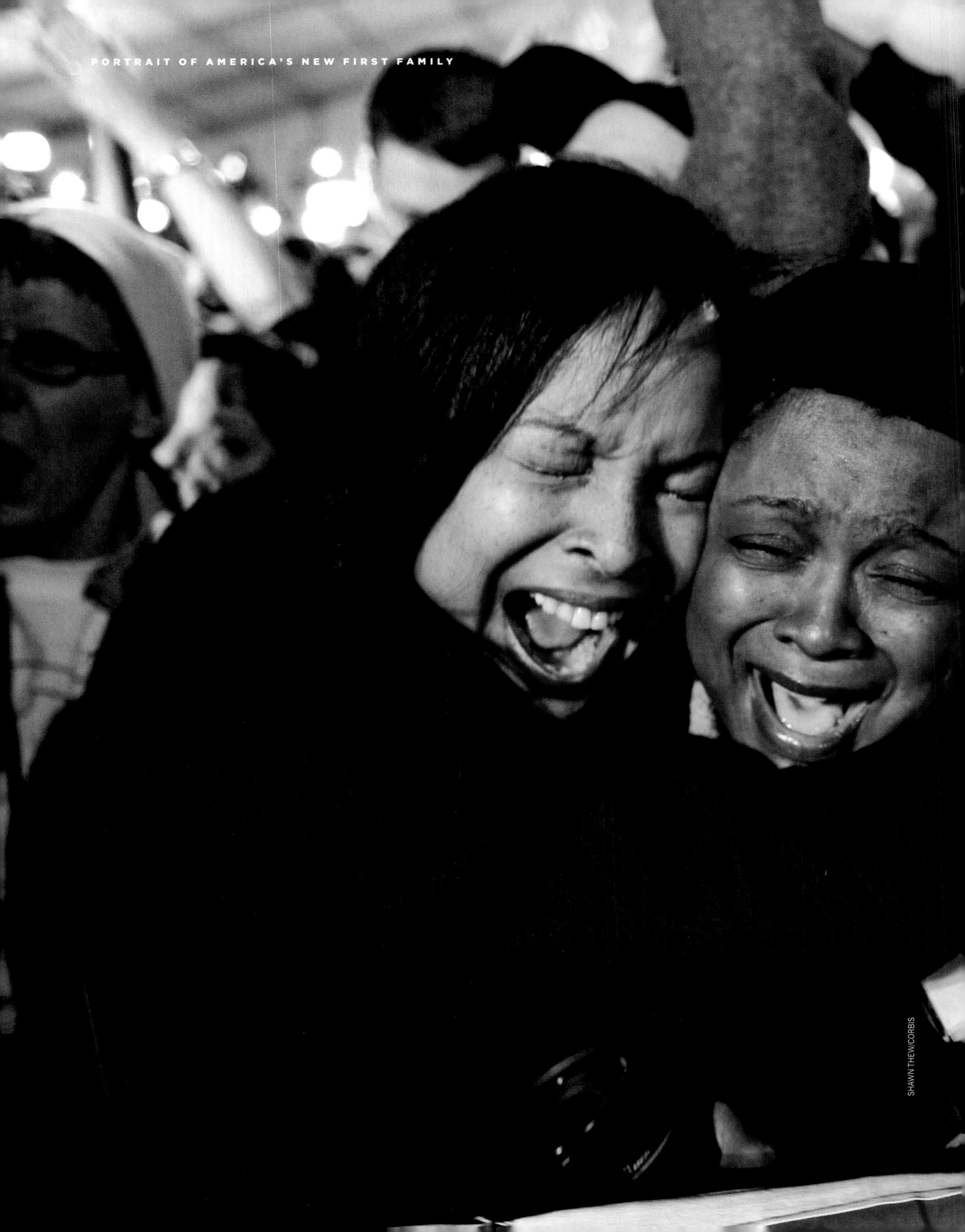

SHAWN THEW/CORBIS

The jubilant crowd in Grant Park in Chicago the night Obama was elected, November 4, 2008.

Why I Voted

TENICIA SPEECH
Jackson, Mississippi

I woke up at 5:00 A.M. I was excited and anxious.
I was in line to vote at 6:20 A.M. with my
63-year-old mother. It took us an hour to vote.
Once we finished, my mother went to pick up
her 91-year-old cousin to take him to vote.
Once she returned, I took my 67-year-old father.
It was one of the most important days of my life.

A PIONEER'S TEARS

By Charlayne Hunter-Gault

I have been sitting for hours glued to the television when suddenly the roomful of people around me erupts with exuberant emotion. I join them, no longer the journalist who observes from a professional distance but a child of the Civil Rights Movement, whose past compelled me to travel some 8,000 miles—from Johannesburg, South Africa, where I live, back to Atlanta. This is the place I needed to be at the moment when Dr. Martin Luther King, Jr.'s dream became reality.

My own history in this city had compelled me to believe it would happen. So I needed to be here, near the grave I will visit tomorrow to thank my mother, Althea Hunter, for her incredible response when I told her many years ago that I dreamed of becoming a reporter "like Brenda Starr." Her reaction belied the reality of the Jim Crow South. She said simply, "If that's what you want to do." On this November night I am shedding tears of gratitude for her and for Dr. King, who affirmed my ambition as he marched here in Atlanta with an army of students that included my two best friends, Wylma and Carolyn Long, who vowed to go to "jail without bail" until there were no more White and colored water fountains.

The Black doctors, lawyers, educators and executives in this room are where they are today because of Wylma's and Carolyn's sacrifice. I think of the comfort those two brave friends gave me when I was a young woman, the only Black student in a college dormitory where a White man who had escaped from an insane asylum came asking for me with a gun in his hand. I shed tears then too, but tears of determination to stay the course. Hamilton Holmes and I, the first Black students at the University of Georgia, set out to prove that we were as good as anyone else. All our tears helped mix the mortar used to build the foundation on which all of us in this room tonight stand. In a few minutes Barack Obama will also acknowledge his debt to those who dreamed of freedom and even died for it. My tears now are of joy for him and the generation that seized the torch we've been holding for them.

Suddenly I find myself needing to hear my friend Wylma's voice, and soon she is on the line, telling me that she, too, has been moved to tears not only by Obama's victory but by her 39-year-old son, Roland, who just hugged her as he thanked her for her sacrifice. And for a while, we are holding the phone, experiencing in silence our proud history.

This article first appeared in the January 2009 issue of ESSENCE.

Obama crosses the Edmund Pettus Bridge in Selma, Alabama, during a reenactment of the historic 1965 Selma-to-Montgomery protest, March 4, 2007.

LEE CELANO REUTERS

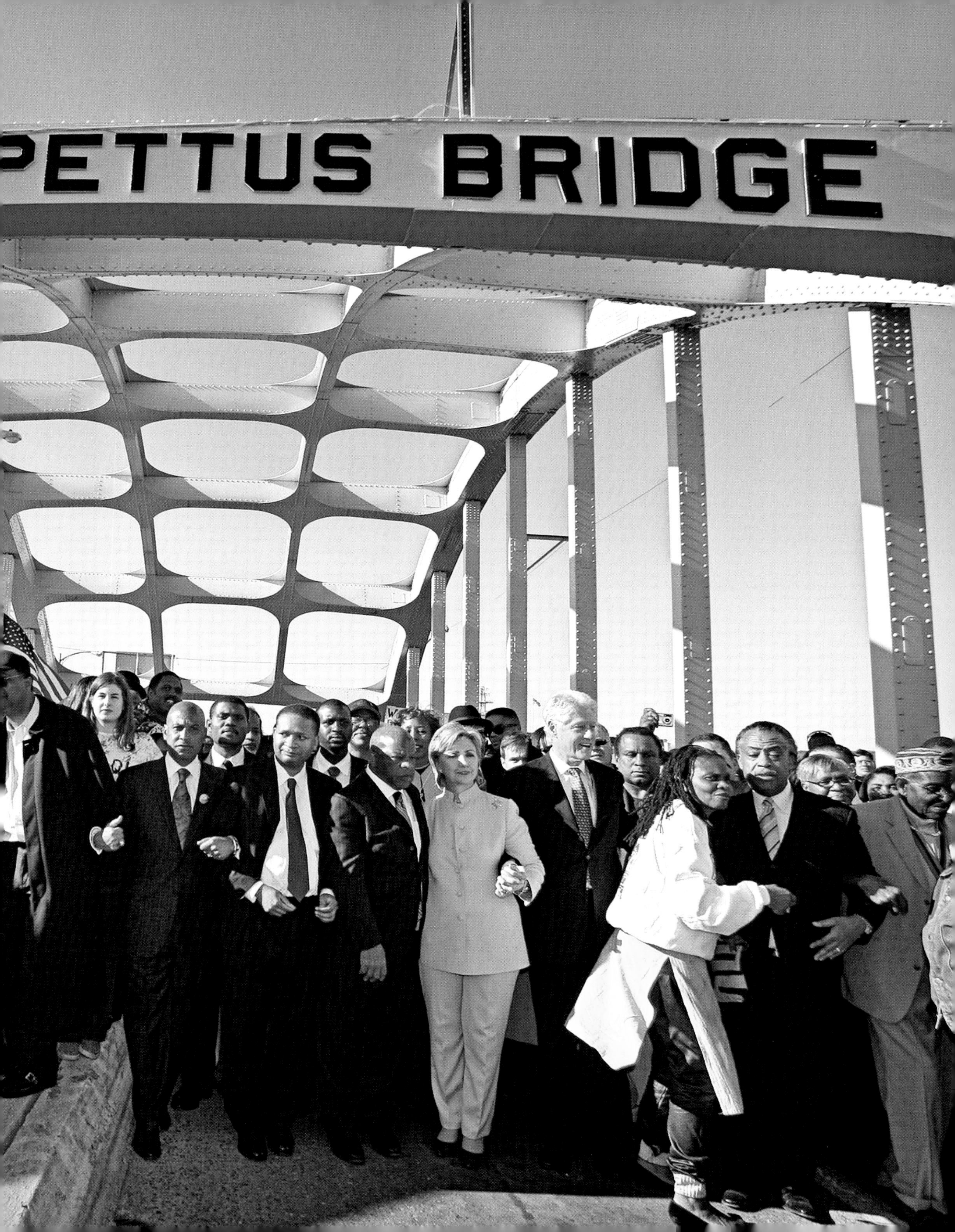
PETTUS BRIDGE

Why I Voted

VALJEANNE JEFFERS-THOMPSON
Durham, North Carolina

I voted early. For the first time in years there was a line. We cheered the first-time voters, including those who voted in the US for the first time. I never thought I'd live to see a Black man successfully run for president in America.

SCOUT TUFANKJIAN/POLARIS

With his family at Beulah Shoesmith Elementary School in Hyde Park, Chicago, Barack holds up the receipt showing he voted.

Why I Voted

RAKISHA KEARNS WHITE
Brooklyn

My voting experience was excellent. I brought my two daughters, who are 1 and 3 years old. We only had to wait in line for about 15 minutes before we were able to get into the polling station. My election district line was short. I signed in and went in to vote. My 3-year-old flipped the switch for Obama, and then my kids and I all pulled the lever together to enter our vote. As we left, I told them that one day they will be able to tell their children how they helped vote for America's first Black president.

At a "watch party," Tyrese Lee (center), 8, of Marshall, Minnesota, holds a sign while he gazes at a large screen showing Obama delivering his victory speech, November 4, 2008.

© 2008 Deeper Arts Inc.

109

Why I Voted

RADIA HASSAN
Chicago

I voted first thing this morning. My polling place is in my building, and when I went down at 5:45 A.M. there was already a line! It took me about 30 minutes. I am so excited because of all that this could mean for so many people. I've volunteered with the campaign, so I am very invested. I've got no ticket to the rally, but I live across the street, so I'll be able to hear and kind of see what's going on. I just may run down and dance in the street with everyone should he win!

Reaching out to touch hope in Lake Worth, Florida, October 21, 2008.

President Barack Obama begins his first full day at work in the Oval Office, January 21, 2009.